Microsoft® Office Excel 2003

ILLUSTRATED

BASIC

(1 of 3)

Elizabeth Eisner Reding • Lynn Wermers

THOMSON
COURSE TECHNOLOGY™

Australia • Canada • Mexico • Singapore • Spain • United Kingdom • United States

Microsoft® Office Excel 2003 - Illustrated Basic

Elizabeth Eisner Reding, Lynn Wermers

Executive Editor:
Nicole Jones Pinard

Production Editor:
Aimee Poirier

QA Manuscript Reviewers:
Alex White, Chris Carvalho

Product Managers:
Christina Kling Garrett,
Jane Hosie-Bounar,
Jeanne Herring

Developmental Editors:
Kim Crowley, Barbara Clemens

Text Designer:
Joseph Lee, Black Fish Design

Associate Product Manager:
Emilie Perreault

Editorial Assistant:
Abbey Reider

Composition House:
GEX Publishing Services

ISBN-13: 978-0-619-05772-5
ISBN-10: 0-619-05772-6

The Illustrated Series Vision

Teaching and writing about computer applications can be extremely rewarding and challenging. How do we engage students and keep their interest? How do we teach them skills that they can easily apply on the job? As we set out to write this book, our goals were to develop a textbook that:

- works for a beginning student

- provides varied, flexible, and meaningful exercises and projects to reinforce the skills

- serves as a reference tool

- makes your job as an educator easier, by providing resources above and beyond the textbook to help you teach your course

Our popular, streamlined format is based on advice from instructional designers and customers. This flexible design presents each lesson on a two-page spread, with step-by-step instructions on the left, and screen illustrations on the right. This signature style, coupled with high-caliber content, provides a comprehensive yet manageable introduction to Microsoft Office Excel 2003—it is a teaching package for the instructor and a learning experience for the student.

Acknowledgments

Creating a book of this magnitude is a team effort. I would like to thank my husband, Michael, as well as Christina Kling Garrett, the project manager who experienced a true baptism-by-fire, Emilie Perreault, associate product manager, and my development editor, Kim Crowley, for her suggestions and corrections. I would also like to thank the production and editorial staff for all their hard work that made this project a reality.

Elizabeth Eisner Reding

I would like to thank Barbara Clemens for her insightful contributions and guidance. I would also like to thank Christina Kling Garrett for patiently answering and researching my endless questions.

Lynn Wermers

Preface

Welcome to *Microsoft Office® Excel 2003–Illustrated Basic*. Each lesson in this book contains elements pictured to the right.

How is the book organized?
The book is organized into five units on Excel, covering creating and editing worksheets, formatting worksheets, working with charts, and using formulas and functions.

What kinds of assignments are included in the book? At what level of difficulty?
The lessons use MediaLoft, a fictional chain of bookstores, as the case study. The assignments on the light purple pages at the end of each unit increase in difficulty. Data files and case studies, with many international examples, provide a great variety of interesting and relevant business applications. Assignments include:

- **Concepts Reviews** include multiple choice, matching, and screen identification questions.

- **Skills Reviews** provide additional hands-on, step-by-step reinforcement.

- **Independent Challenges** are case projects requiring critical thinking and application of the unit skills. The Independent Challenges increase in difficulty, with the first one in each unit being the easiest (most step-by-step with detailed instructions). Independent Challenges 2 and 3 become increasingly open-ended, requiring more independent problem solving.

- **E-Quest Independent Challenges** are case projects with a Web focus. E-Quests require the use of the World Wide Web to conduct research to complete the project.

- **Advanced Challenge Exercises** set within the Independent Challenges provide optional steps for more advanced students.

- **Visual Workshops** are practical, self-graded capstone projects that require independent problem solving.

Each 2-page spread focuses on a single skill.

Concise text introduces the basic principles in the lesson and integrates a real-world case study.

UNIT C
Excel 2003

Applying Colors, Patterns, and Borders

You can use colors, patterns, and borders to enhance the overall appearance of a worksheet and to make it easier to read. You can add these enhancements by using the Patterns or Borders tabs in the Format Cells dialog box or by using the Borders and Color buttons on the Formatting toolbar. You can apply color or patterns to the background of a cell, to a range, or to cell contents. You can also apply borders to all the cells in a worksheet or only to selected cells to call attention to individual cells or groups of cells. See Table C-4 for a list of border buttons and their functions. ▶▶▶▶ Jim asks you to add a pattern, a border, and color to the title of the worksheet to give the worksheet a more professional appearance.

STEPS

1. **Press [Ctrl][Home] to select cell** A1, **then click the** Fill Color list arrow **on the Formatting toolbar**
   The color palette appears.

> **QUICK TIP**
> Use color sparingly. Too much color can divert the reader's attention from the worksheet data.

2. **Click the** Turquoise color **(fourth row, fifth column)**
   Cell A1 has a turquoise background, as shown in Figure C-14. Cell A1 spans columns A through I because of the Merge and Center command used for the title.

3. **Right-click cell** A1, **then click** Format Cells **on the shortcut menu**
   The Format Cells dialog box opens.

4. **Click the** Patterns tab **if it is not already displayed**
   See Figure C-15. Adding a pattern to cells can add to the visual interest of your worksheet.

> **QUICK TIP**
> You can also draw cell borders using the mouse pointer. Click the Borders list arrow on the Formatting toolbar, click Draw Borders, then drag to create borders or boxes.

5. **Click the** Pattern list arrow, **click the** Thin Diagonal Crosshatch pattern **(third row, last column), then click** OK
   A border also enhances a cell's appearance. Unlike underlining, which is a text-formatting tool, borders extend to the width of the cell.

6. **Click the** Borders list arrow **on the Formatting toolbar, then click the** Thick Bottom Border **(second row, second column)** **on the Borders palette**
   It can be difficult to view a border in a selected cell.

7. **Click cell** A3
   The border is a nice enhancement. Font color can also help distinguish information in a worksheet.

> **QUICK TIP**
> The default color on the Fill Color and Font Color buttons changes to the last color you selected.

8. **Select the range** A3:I3, **click the** Font Color list arrow **on the Formatting toolbar, then click the** Blue **color (second row, third column from the right) on the palette**
   The text changes color, as shown in Figure C-16.

9. **Click the** Save button **on the Standard toolbar**

Clues to Use

Formatting columns or rows
You can save yourself time by formatting an entire column or row using any of the categories that appear in the Format Cells dialog box. You might, for example, want to format all the cells within a column to accept telephone numbers, social security numbers, zip codes, or custom number formats. Click the column or row heading—located at the top of a column or beginning of a row—to select the entire column or row. You can format a selected column or row by clicking Format on the menu bar, clicking Cells, then clicking the appropriate tab in the Format Cells dialog box.

EXCEL C-12 FORMATTING A WORKSHEET

OFFICE-262

Tips, as well as troubleshooting advice, right where you need them—next to the step itself.

Clues to Use boxes provide concise information that either expands on the major lesson skill or describes an independent task that in some way relates to the major lesson skill.

Every lesson features large, full-color representations of what the screen should look like as students complete the numbered steps.

Brightly colored tabs indicate which section of the book you are in.

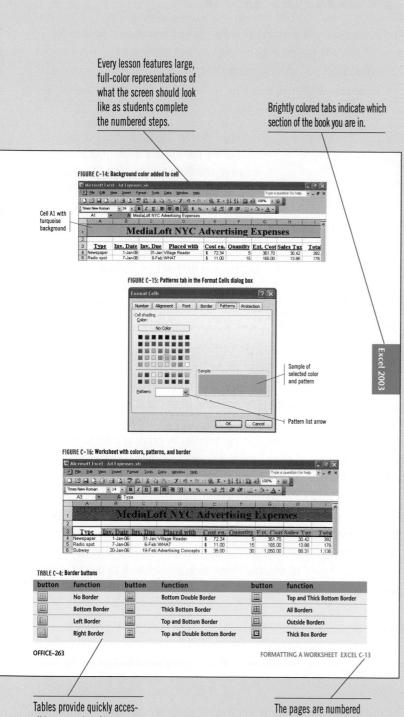

Cell A1 with turquoise background

FIGURE C-14: Background color added to cell

FIGURE C-15: Patterns tab in the Format Cells dialog box

Sample of selected color and pattern

Pattern list arrow

FIGURE C-16: Worksheet with colors, patterns, and border

TABLE C-4: Border buttons

button	function	button	function	button	function
	No Border		Bottom Double Border		Top and Thick Bottom Border
	Bottom Border		Thick Bottom Border		All Borders
	Left Border		Top and Bottom Border		Outside Borders
	Right Border		Top and Double Bottom Border		Thick Box Border

FORMATTING A WORKSHEET EXCEL C-13

Tables provide quickly accessible summaries of key terms, toolbar buttons, or keyboard alternatives connected with the lesson material. Students can refer easily to this information when working on their own projects at a later time.

The pages are numbered according to section and unit. Excel indicates the section, C indicates the unit, 13 indicates the page.

What online content solutions are available to accompany this book?

Visit www.course.com for more information on our online content for Illustrated titles. Options include:

MyCourse 2.0

Need a quick, simple tool to help you manage your course? Try MyCourse 2.0, the easiest to use, most flexible syllabus and content management tool available. MyCourse 2.0 offers you brand new content, including Topic Reviews, Extra Case Projects, and Quizzes, to accompany this book.

WebCT

Course Technology and WebCT have partnered to provide you with the highest quality online resources and Web-based tools for your class. Course Technology offers content for this book to help you create your WebCT class, such as a suggested Syllabus, Lecture Notes, Practice Test questions, and more.

Blackboard

Course Technology and Blackboard have also partnered to provide you with the highest quality online resources and Web-based tools for your class. Course Technology offers content for this book to help you create your Blackboard class, such as a suggested Syllabus, Lecture Notes, Practice Test questions, and more.

Is this book Microsoft Office Specialist Certified?

When used in conjunction with *Microsoft Office Excel 2003 – Illustrated Intermediate*, this book covers the objectives for Microsoft Office Excel 2003. When used in conjunction with *Microsoft Office Excel 2003 – Illustrated Intermediate* and *Advanced*, this book covers the objectives for Microsoft Office Excel 2003 and Microsoft Office Excel 2003 Expert. When used in this sequence, these titles have received certification approval as courseware for the Microsoft Office Specialist program. See the inside front cover for more information on other Illustrated titles meeting Microsoft Office Specialist certification.

The first page of each unit indicates which objectives in the unit are Microsoft Office Specialist skills. If an objective is set in red, it meets a Microsoft Office Specialist skill. A document on the CD accompanying this book cross-references the skills with the lessons and exercises.

v

Instructor Resources

The Instructor Resources CD is Course Technology's way of putting the resources and information needed to teach and learn effectively into your hands. With an integrated array of teaching and learning tools that offers you and your students a broad range of technology-based instructional options, we believe this CD represents the highest quality and most cutting edge resources available to instructors today. Many of these resources are available at www.course.com. The resources available with this book are:

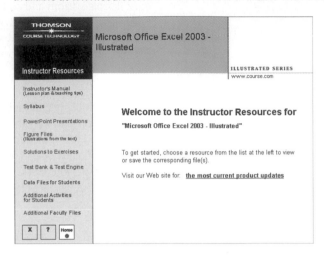

- **Data Files for Students**—To complete most of the units in this book, your students will need the **Data Files** on the CD in the back of this book. The Data Files are also available on the Instructor Resources CD and can be downloaded from www.course.com.

Instruct students to use the **Data Files List** located on the CD. This list gives instructions on copying and organizing files.

- **Solutions to Exercises**—Solutions to Exercises contains every file students are asked to create or modify in the lessons and End-of-Unit material. A Help file on the Instructor Resources CD includes information for using the Solution Files. There is also a document outlining the solutions for the End-of-Unit Concepts Review, Skills Review, and Independent Challenges.

- **PowerPoint Presentations**—Each unit has a corresponding PowerPoint presentation that you can use in a lecture, distribute to your students, or customize to suit your course.

- **Instructor's Manual**—Available as an electronic file, the Instructor's Manual is quality-assurance tested and includes unit overviews, and detailed lecture topics with teaching tips for each unit.

- **Sample Syllabus**—Prepare and customize your course easily using this sample course outline.

- **Figure Files**—The figures in the text are provided on the Instructor Resources CD to help you illustrate key topics or concepts. You can create traditional overhead transparencies by printing the figure files. Or you can create electronic slide shows by using the figures in a presentation program such as PowerPoint.

- **ExamView**—ExamView is a powerful testing software package that allows you to create and administer printed, computer (LAN-based), and Internet exams. ExamView includes hundreds of questions that correspond to the topics covered in this text, enabling students to generate detailed study guides that include page references for further review. The computer-based and Internet testing components allow students to take exams at their computers, and also saves you time by grading each exam automatically.

SAM 2003 Assessment & Training

SAM 2003 helps you energize your class exams and training assignments by allowing students to learn and test important computer skills in an active, hands-on environment.

With SAM 2003 Assessment, you create powerful interactive exams on critical applications such as Word, Outlook, PowerPoint, Windows, the Internet, and much more. The exams simulate the application environment, allowing your students to demonstrate their knowledge and think through the skills by performing real-world tasks.

Designed to be used with the Illustrated series, SAM 2003 Assessment & Training includes built-in page references so students can create study guides that match the Illustrated textbooks you use in class. Powerful administrative options allow you to schedule exams and assignments, secure your tests, and run reports with almost limitless flexibility.

Contents

Read This Before You Begin

Software Information and Required Installation

This book was written and tested using Microsoft Office 2003 - Professional Edition, with a typical installation on Microsoft Windows XP plus installation of the latest Service Pack, and with Internet Explorer 6.0 or higher. Some of the exercises in this book assume that your computer is connected to the Internet. If you are not connected to the Internet, see your instructor for information.

Tips for Students

What are Data Files?

To complete many of the units in this book, you need to use Data Files from the CD in the back of this book. A Data File contains a partially completed document, so that you don't have to type in all the information in the document yourself. Your instructor can give you instructions on how to organize your files, as well as a complete file listing, or you can find the list and the instructions for organizing your files on the CD.

Why is my screen different from the book?

Your Desktop components and some dialog box options might be different if you are using an operating system other than Windows XP.

Depending on your computer hardware and the display settings on your computer, you may also notice the following differences:

- Your screen may look larger or smaller because of your screen resolution (the height and width of your screen).

- Your title bars and dialog boxes may not display file extensions. To display file extensions, click Start on the taskbar, click Control Panel, click Appearance and Themes, then click Folder Options. Click the View tab if necessary, click Hide extensions for known file types to deselect it, then click OK. Your Office dialog boxes and title bars should now display file extensions.

- The colors of the title bar in your screen may be a solid blue, and the cells in Excel may appear different from the orange and gray because of your color settings

- Depending on your Office settings, your toolbars may be displayed on a single row and your menus may display a shortened list of frequently used commands. Office menus and toolbars can modify themselves to your working style by displaying only the most frequently used buttons and menu commands. To view buttons not currently displayed, click a Toolbar Options button █ at the end of either the Standard or Formatting toolbar. To view the full list of menu commands, click the double arrow at the bottom of the menu.

Toolbars in one row

Toolbars in two rows

In order to have your toolbars displayed in two rows, showing all buttons, and to have the full menus displayed, you must turn off the personalized menus and toolbars feature. Click Tools on the menu bar, click Customize, select the show Standard and Formatting toolbars on two rows and Always show full menus check boxes on the Options tab, and then click Close. This book assumes you are displaying toolbars in two rows and displaying full menus.

Getting Started with Excel 2003

OBJECTIVES

| Define spreadsheet software |
| Start Excel 2003 |
| View the Excel window |
| Open and save a workbook |
| Enter labels and values |
| Name and move a sheet |
| Preview and print a worksheet |
| Get Help |
| Close a workbook and exit Excel |

If you have a SAM user profile, you may have access to hands-on instruction, practice, and assessment of the skills covered in this unit. Log in to your SAM account and go to your assignments page to see what your instructor has assigned.

In this unit, you will learn how to start Microsoft Office Excel 2003 and identify elements in the Excel window. You will also learn how to open and save existing files, enter data in a worksheet, manipulate worksheets, and use the extensive Help system. Jim Fernandez is the office manager at MediaLoft, a chain of bookstore cafés founded in 1988. MediaLoft stores offer customers the opportunity to purchase books, music, and movies while enjoying a variety of coffees, teas, and freshly baked desserts. Jim wants you, his assistant, to learn how to use Excel and help him analyze a worksheet summarizing budget information for the MediaLoft café in the New York City location.

Defining Spreadsheet Software

Microsoft Excel is an electronic spreadsheet program that runs on Windows computers. You use an **electronic spreadsheet** to produce professional-looking documents that perform numeric calculations rapidly and accurately. These calculations are updated automatically so that accurate information is always available. See Table A-1 for common ways spreadsheets are used in business. The electronic spreadsheet that you produce when using Excel is also referred to as a **worksheet**. Individual worksheets are stored within a **workbook**, which is a file with the .xls file extension. Each new workbook automatically contains three worksheets, although you can have up to 255 sheets. ██████ Jim uses Excel extensively to track MediaLoft finances, and as you work with Jim, you will also use Excel to complete many tasks. Figure A-1 shows a budget worksheet that Jim created using pencil and paper, while Figure A-2 shows the same worksheet Jim created using Excel.

DETAILS

When you use Excel you have the ability to:

- **Enter data quickly and accurately**

    With Excel, you can enter information faster and more accurately than with pencil and paper. For example, in the MediaLoft NYC Café Budget, certain expenses, such as rent, cleaning supplies, and products supplied on a yearly contract (coffee, creamers, and sweeteners), remain constant for the year. You can copy the expenses that don't change from quarter to quarter, then use Excel to calculate Total Expenses and Net Income for each quarter by supplying the data and formulas.

- **Recalculate data easily**

    Fixing typing errors or updating data using Excel is easy, and the results of a changed entry are recalculated automatically. For example, if you receive updated expense figures for Quarter 4, you enter the new numbers, and Excel recalculates the worksheet.

- **Perform a what-if analysis**

    The ability in Excel to change data and quickly view the recalculated results makes it a powerful decision-making tool. For instance, if the salary budget per quarter is increased to $17,200, you can enter the new figure into the worksheet and immediately see the impact on the overall budget. Any time you use a worksheet to ask the question "what if?" you are performing a **what-if analysis**.

- **Change the appearance of information**

    Excel provides powerful features for making information visually appealing and easy to understand. For example, you can use boldface type and colored or shaded text headings or numbers to emphasize important worksheet data and trends.

- **Create charts**

    Excel makes it easy to create charts based on worksheet information. Charts are updated automatically as data changes. The worksheet in Figure A-2 includes a 3-D pie chart that shows the distribution of the budget expenses for the MediaLoft NYC Café.

- **Share information with other users**

    Because everyone at MediaLoft is now using Microsoft Office, it's easy for them to share worksheet data. For example, you can complete the MediaLoft budget that Jim started creating in Excel. Simply access the files you need or want to share through the network or from a disk, or through the use of online collaboration tools (such as intranets and the Internet), and make any changes or additions.

- **Create new worksheets from existing ones quickly**

    It's easy to take an existing Excel worksheet and quickly modify it to create a new one. When you are ready to create next year's budget, you can open the file for this year's budget, save it with a new filename, and use the existing data as a starting point. An Excel file can also be created using a special format called a **template**, which lets you open a new file based on an existing workbook's design or content. Excel comes with many prepared templates you can use.

FIGURE A-1: Traditional paper worksheet

MediaLoft NYC Café Budget

	Qtr 1	Qtr 2	Qtr 3	Qtr 4	Total
Net Sales	56,000	84,000	72,000	79,000	291,000
Expenses					
Salary	17,200	17,200	17,200	17,200	68,800
Rent	4,000	4,000	4,000	4,000	16,000
Advertising	3,750	8,000	3,750	3,750	19,250
Cleansers	2,200	2,200	2,200	2,200	8,800
Pastries	2,500	2,500	2,500	2,500	10,000
Milk/Cream	1,000	1,000	1,000	1,000	4,000
Coffee/Tea	4,700	4,750	4,750	4,750	18,950
Sweeteners	650	650	650	650	2,600
Total Expenses	36,000	40,300	36,050	36,050	148,400
Net Income	20,000	43,700	35,950	42,950	142,600

FIGURE A-2: Excel worksheet

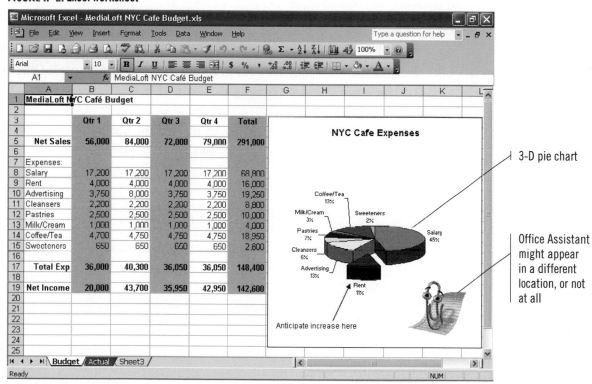

3-D pie chart

Office Assistant might appear in a different location, or not at all

TABLE A-1: Common business uses for electronic spreadsheets

spreadsheets are used to	by
Maintain values	Calculating numbers
Represent values graphically	Creating charts based on worksheet figures
Create reports to summarize data	Creating workbooks containing multiple worksheets of related data, and numbering and printing the worksheets as consecutively numbered pages
Organize data	Sorting data in ascending or descending order
Analyze data	Creating data summaries and short lists using PivotTables or AutoFilters
Create what-if data scenarios	Using variable values to investigate and sample different outcomes

UNIT A
Excel 2003

Starting Excel 2003

To start any Windows program, you use the Start button on the taskbar. A slightly different procedure might be required for computers on a network and those that use Windows-enhancing utilities. If you need assistance, ask your instructor or technical support person. Jim has asked you to work on the budget for the MediaLoft café in New York City, which he created using Excel. You begin by starting Excel.

STEPS

1. **Point to the Start button** 🏁 start **on the taskbar**

   The Start button is on the left side of the taskbar. You use it to start programs on your computer.

> **QUICK TIP**
> You might also see Microsoft Office Excel 2003 listed on the left side of the Start menu, which you can also click to start Excel.

2. **Click** 🏁 start

   Microsoft Office Excel is located on the All Programs menu, which is located at the bottom of the Start menu, as shown in Figure A-3.

3. **Point to All Programs**

   The All Programs menu opens. All the programs on your computer, including Microsoft Excel, are listed on this menu. Your All Programs menu might look different, depending on the programs installed on your computer.

4. **Point to Microsoft Office**

   A submenu displays listing all the Microsoft Office programs installed on your computer. See Figure A-4.

> **TROUBLE**
> If you don't see the Microsoft Office Excel 2003 icon, see your instructor or technical support person.

5. **Click the Microsoft Office Excel 2003 program icon on the Microsoft Office submenu**

   Excel opens and a blank worksheet is displayed. In the next lesson, you will learn about the elements of the Excel worksheet window.

6. **If necessary, click the Maximize button** 🔲 **on the title bar**

   In the next lesson, you will learn about the elements of the Excel worksheet window.

FIGURE A-3: Start menu

Microsoft Office Excel located on this menu

Click here to open the Start menu

Your list might differ

FIGURE A-4: All Programs menu

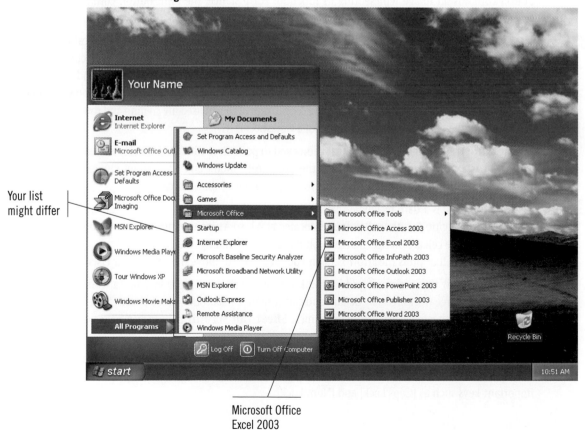

Your list might differ

Microsoft Office Excel 2003 program icon

Excel 2003

UNIT
A

Excel 2003

Viewing the Excel Window

When you start Excel, the worksheet window appears on your screen. The **worksheet window** includes the tools that enable you to create and work with worksheets. ▰▰▰▰▰ You need to familiarize yourself with the Excel worksheet window and its elements before you start working on the budget worksheet. Compare the descriptions below to the elements shown in Figure A-5.

DETAILS

The elements of the Excel worksheet window include:

QUICK TIP

There are two sets of resizing buttons: one for the program and another for the active workbook. The program's resizing buttons are located on the title bar, while the workbook's resizing buttons appear below the program resizing buttons, on the menu bar (when the workbook is maximized).

- The **title bar** displays the program name (Microsoft Excel) and the filename of the open worksheet (in this case the default filename, Book1). As shown in Figure A-5, the title bar also contains a control menu box, a Close button, and resizing buttons, which are common to all Windows programs. The **control menu box** provides a menu of commands that allow you to move, size, open, or close the program window.

- The **menu bar** contains menus from which you select Excel commands. As with all Windows programs, you can select a menu command by clicking it with the mouse pointer or by pressing [Alt] plus the underlined letter in the menu command name. When you click a menu, only a short list of commonly used commands might appear at first; you can wait or click the double arrows at the bottom of the menu to see expanded menus with a complete list of commands.

- The **Name box** displays the active cell address. In Figure A-5, "A1" appears in the Name box, indicating that A1 is the active cell.

- The **formula bar** allows you to enter or edit data in the worksheet.

- The **toolbars** contain buttons for frequently used Excel commands. The **Standard toolbar** is located just below the menu bar and contains buttons that perform actions within the worksheet. The **Formatting toolbar**—beneath the Standard toolbar—contains buttons that change the worksheet's appearance. Each button contains an image representing its function. For instance, the Print button contains an image of a printer. To select any button, click it with the left mouse button.

QUICK TIP

You can always return to the Getting Started task pane by clicking the Home button 🏠 at the top of any task pane.

- The worksheet window contains a grid of columns and rows. Columns are labeled alphabetically (A, B, C, etc.) and rows are labeled numerically (1, 2, 3, etc.). The worksheet window displays only a small fraction of the whole worksheet, which has a total of 256 columns and 65,536 rows. The intersection of a column and a row is called a **cell**. Cells can contain text, numbers, formulas, or a combination of all three. Every cell has its own unique location or **cell address**, which is identified by the coordinates of the intersecting column and row. For example, the cell address of the cell in the upper-left corner of a worksheet is A1.

- A **task pane** is an organizational tool that allows you to perform routine tasks quickly and easily. The **Getting Started task pane** appears to the right of the worksheet window and lets you quickly open new or existing workbooks. The **Task pane list arrow** lets you choose from 12 different panes.

TROUBLE

If your screen does not display cells in orange and gray as shown in the figure, ask your technical support person to check your Windows color settings.

- The **cell pointer** is a dark rectangle that outlines the cell in which you are working. This cell is called the **active cell**. In Figure A-5, the cell pointer is located at A1, so A1 is the active cell. The column and row headings for the active cell are orange; inactive column and row headings are gray. To activate a different cell, just click any other cell or press the arrow keys on your keyboard to move the cell pointer elsewhere.

- **Sheet tabs** below the worksheet grid let you keep your work in a collection called a workbook. Each workbook contains three worksheets by default and can contain a maximum of 255 sheets. Sheet tabs allow you to name your worksheets with meaningful names. **Sheet tab scrolling buttons** help you display hidden worksheets.

- The **status bar** is located at the bottom of the Excel window. The left side of the status bar provides a brief description of the active command or task in progress. The right side of the status bar shows the status of important keys such as [Caps Lock] and [Num Lock].

FIGURE A-5: Excel worksheet window elements

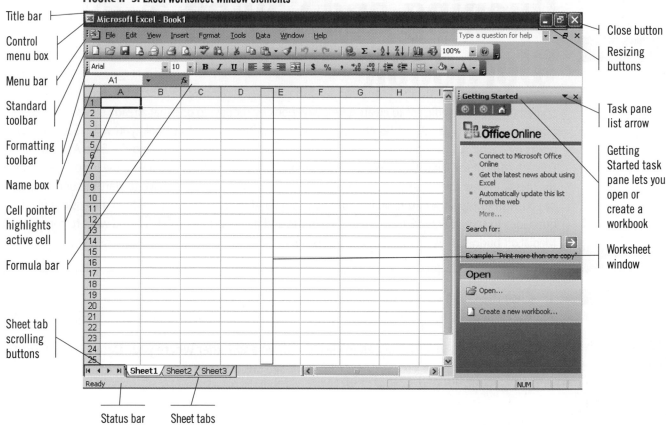

Title bar
Control menu box
Menu bar
Standard toolbar
Formatting toolbar
Name box
Cell pointer highlights active cell
Formula bar
Sheet tab scrolling buttons

Close button
Resizing buttons
Task pane list arrow
Getting Started task pane lets you open or create a workbook
Worksheet window

Status bar   Sheet tabs

Clues to Use

Working with toolbars and menus in Excel 2003

Although you can configure Excel so that your toolbars and menus modify themselves to conform to your working style, the lessons in this book assume you have turned off personalized menus and toolbars and are working with all menu commands and toolbar buttons displayed. When you use personalized toolbars, the Standard and Formatting toolbars appear on the same row and display only the most frequently used buttons, as shown in Figure A-6. To use a button that is not visible on a toolbar, you click the Toolbar Options button at the end of the toolbar, then click the button on the Toolbar Options list. As you work, Excel adds the buttons you use to the visible toolbars and drops the buttons you don't often use to the Toolbar Options list. Similarly, Excel menus adjust to your work habits, so that

the commands you use most often appear on shortened menus. You can see all the menu commands by clicking the Expand button (double arrows) at the bottom of a menu. It is often easier to work with full toolbars and menus displayed. To turn off personalized toolbars and menus, click Tools on the menu bar, click Customize, then click the Options tab in the Customize dialog box. Select the Show Standard and Formatting toolbars on two rows and Always show full menus check boxes, then click Close. The Standard and Formatting toolbars appear on separate rows and display most of the buttons, and the menus display the complete list of menu commands. (You can also quickly display the toolbars on two rows by clicking a Toolbar Options button, then clicking Show Buttons on Two Rows.)

FIGURE A-6: Toolbars on one row

Toolbar Options buttons

Opening and Saving a Workbook

Sometimes it's more efficient to create a new workbook by modifying one that already exists. This saves you from having to retype information from previous work. Throughout this book, you will create new workbooks by opening a file from the location where your Data Files are stored, using the Save As command to create a copy of the file with a new name, then modifying the new file by following the lesson steps. Saving the files with new names keeps your original Data Files intact, in case you have to start the unit over again or you wish to repeat an exercise. Use the Save command to store changes made to an existing file. It is a good idea to save your work every 10 or 15 minutes and before printing. ▰▰▰▰ You want to complete the MediaLoft budget on which Jim has been working.

STEPS

QUICK TIP

If the task pane is not open, click View on the menu bar, then click Task Pane to display the Getting Started task pane.

1. **Click the Open button 🗁 in the Getting Started task pane**

   The Open dialog box opens. See Figure A-7. You can also click the Open button 🗁 on the Standard toolbar.

2. **Click the Look in list arrow, then click the drive and folder where your Data Files are located**

   The Look in list arrow lets you navigate to folders and disk drives on your computer. A list of your Data Files appears in the Open dialog box.

QUICK TIP

If you don't see the three-letter extension .xls on the filenames in the Open dialog box, don't worry. Windows can be set up to display or not to display the file extensions.

3. **Click the file EX A-1.xls, then click Open**

   The file EX A-1.xls opens. The Getting Started task pane no longer appears on the screen.

4. **Click File on the menu bar, then click Save As**

   The Save As dialog box opens, displaying the drive where your Data Files are stored. You can create a new folder from within the Save As dialog box by clicking 🗀 on the dialog box toolbar, typing a name in the Name text box, then clicking OK. To open a file from a folder you create, double-click folders, or use the Look in list arrow in the Open dialog box to open the folder, click the filename, then click Open.

5. **In the File name text box, select the current filename if necessary, type MediaLoft Cafe Budget, as shown in Figure A-8, then click Save**

   Both the Save As dialog box and the file EX A-1.xls close, and a duplicate file named MediaLoft Cafe Budget opens, as shown in Figure A-9.

Clues to Use

Creating a new workbook

You can create your own worksheets from scratch by opening a new workbook. To create a new workbook, click the New button 🗋 on the Standard toolbar. You can also use the Getting Started or New Workbook task panes to open a new workbook. Click the Go to New Workbook task pane button 🗋 in the Getting Started task pane to open the New Workbook task pane, then click the Blank Workbook button 🗋 to open a new workbook.

FIGURE A-7: Open dialog box

My Documents
folder opens
by default

Your files and
folders appear
here; your
contents
might differ

Selected
filename will
appear here

Look in
list arrow

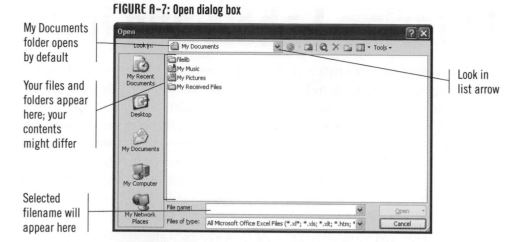

FIGURE A-8: Save As dialog box

Current drive
or folder (yours
might differ)

Your list of
files might
differ

Type new
filename
here

FIGURE A-9: MediaLoft Café Budget workbook

Orange column
and row headers
define the
active cell

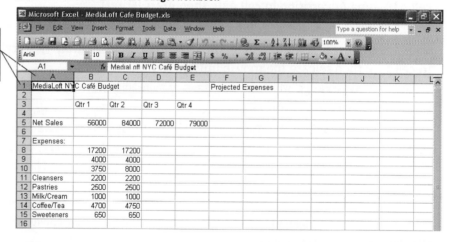

Clues to Use

Opening a workbook using a template

You can create a workbook by entering data and formats into a blank workbook, or you can use predesigned workbooks called templates that are included with Excel. Templates let you automatically create workbooks such as balance sheets, expense statements, loan amortizations, sales invoices, or timecards. Templates save you time because they contain labels, values, formulas, and formatting. To open a new workbook based on a template, click the Other Task Panes list arrow from the Getting Started task pane, then click New Workbook. Click the On my computer link under the Templates section, then click the Spreadsheet Solutions tab in the Templates dialog box. Click one of the samples, save it under a new name, then add your own information. You may need to have the Office CD available to install the templates. You can also find more templates by clicking the Templates home page link.

Entering Labels and Values

Labels help you identify the data in worksheet rows and columns, making your worksheet more readable and understandable. You should try to enter all labels in your worksheet before entering the data. Labels can contain text and numerical information not used in calculations, such as dates, times, or addresses. Labels are left-aligned by default. **Values**, which include numbers, formulas, and functions, are used in calculations. Excel recognizes an entry as a value when it is a number, or begins with one of these special symbols: +, -, =, @, #, or $. All values are right-aligned by default. When you ask Excel to total data in a column, it ignores those cells that have numbers within labels (such as 2006 Sales), and only totals those cells that contain values. When a cell contains both text and numbers, Excel recognizes the entry as a label. You notice that Jim's budget worksheet is missing some data. You want to enter labels identifying the rest of the expense categories, and the values for Qtr 3 and Qtr 4 into the MediaLoft Café Budget worksheet.

STEPS

1. **Click cell A8 to make it the active cell**

   Notice that the cell address A8 appears in the Name box. As you work, the mouse pointer takes on a variety of appearances, depending on where it is and what the program is doing. Table A-2 lists and identifies some mouse pointers. The labels in cells A8:A15 identify the expenses.

   TROUBLE

   If you notice a mistake in a cell entry after entering it, double-click the cell, use [Backspace] or [Delete], make your corrections, then press [Enter]. You can also click Edit on the menu bar, point to Clear, then click Contents to remove a cell's contents.

2. **Type Salary, as shown in Figure A-10, then click the Enter button ✓ on the formula bar**

   As you type, the word "Enter" appears in the status bar. Clicking the Enter button indicates that you are finished typing or changing your entry, and the word "Ready" appears in the status bar. Because the cell is still selected, its contents still appear in the formula bar. You can also confirm a cell entry by pressing [Enter], [Tab], or one of the keyboard arrow keys. These three methods also select an adjacent cell. To confirm an entry and leave the same cell selected, you can press [Ctrl][Enter]. If a label does not fit in a cell, Excel displays the remaining characters in the next cell to the right, as long as it is empty. Otherwise, the label is **truncated**, or cut off.

3. **Click cell A9, type Rent, press [Enter] to confirm the entry and move the cell pointer to cell A10, type Advertising in cell A10, then press [Enter]**

   The remaining expense values have to be added to the worksheet for Quarters 3 and 4.

4. **Click cell D8, press and hold down the left mouse button, drag ✛ to cell E8 then down to cell E15, then release the mouse button**

   You have selected a **range**, which consists of two or more adjacent cells. The active cell is still cell D8, and the cells in the range are shaded in blue.

   QUICK TIP

   To enter a number that will not be used as part of a calculation, such as a telephone number, type an apostrophe (') before the number.

5. **Type 17200, press [Enter], type 4000 in cell D9, press [Enter], type 3750 in cell D10, press [Enter], type 2200 in cell D11, press [Enter], type 2500 in cell D12, press [Enter], type 1000 in cell D13, press [Enter], type 4750 in cell D14, press [Enter], type 650 in cell D15, then press [Enter]**

   You often enter data in multiple columns and rows; selecting a range makes working with data entry easier because pressing [Enter] makes the next cell in the range active. You have entered all the values in the Qtr 3 column. The cell pointer is now in cell E8.

   QUICK TIP

   The **AutoCalculate value** displays the sum of the selected values in the status bar.

6. **Type the remaining values for cells E8 through E15 as shown in Figure A-11**

   Before confirming a cell entry, you can click the Cancel button on the formula bar or press [Esc] to cancel or delete the entry.

7. **Click cell D8, type 17250, then press [Enter]**

8. **Press [Ctrl][Home] to return to cell A1**

9. **Click the Save button 🖫 on the Standard toolbar**

   You can also press [Ctrl][S] to save a worksheet.

FIGURE A-10: Worksheet with first label entered

Name box

Cancel button

Enter button

Formula bar

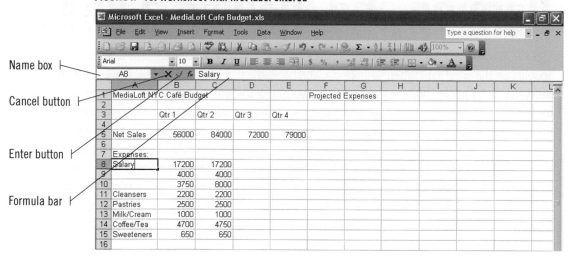

FIGURE A-11: Worksheet with new labels and values

Type these values

Labels entered

Values entered

AutoCalculate value

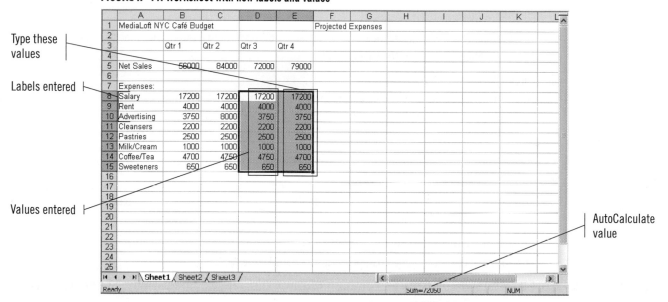

TABLE A-2: Commonly used pointers

name	pointer	use to
Normal	⬩	Select a cell or range; indicates Ready mode
Copy	⬩	Create a duplicate of the selected cell(s)
Fill handle	✚	Create an alphanumeric series in a range
I-beam	I	Edit contents of formula bar
Move	⬩	Change the location of the selected cell(s)

Clues to Use

Navigating a worksheet

With over a million cells available to you, it is important to know how to move around, or navigate, a worksheet. You can use the arrow keys on the keyboard (↑, ↓, ←, or →) to move a cell at a time, or use [Page Up] or [Page Down] to move a screen at a time. To move a screen to the left press [Alt][Page Up]; to move a screen to the right press [Alt][Page Down]. You can also use the mouse pointer to click the desired cell. If the desired cell is not visible in the worksheet window, use the scroll bars or the Go To command on the Edit menu to move the location into view. To return to the first cell in a worksheet, click cell A1, or press [Ctrl][Home].

Excel 2003

Naming and Moving a Sheet

Each workbook initially contains three worksheets, named Sheet1, Sheet2, and Sheet3. The sheet name appears on the sheet tab. When you open a workbook, the first worksheet is the active sheet. To move from sheet to sheet, you can click any sheet tab at the bottom of the worksheet window. The sheet tab scrolling buttons, located to the left of the sheet tabs, allow you to display hidden sheet tabs. To make it easier to identify the sheets in a workbook, you can rename each sheet and add color to the tabs. You can also organize them in a logical way. For instance, to better track performance goals, you could name each workbook sheet for an individual salesperson; then you could move the sheets so they appeared in alphabetical order. You have added data to Sheet1 of the budget workbook, which contains information on projected expenses. Jim tells you that Sheet2 contains data for the actual expenses. You want to be able to easily identify the actual expenses and the projected expenses, so you want to name the two sheets in the workbook, add color to distinguish them, then change their order.

STEPS

1. **Click the Sheet2 tab**

   Sheet2 becomes active; this is the worksheet that contains the actual quarterly expenses. Its tab moves to the front, and Sheet1 moves to the background.

2. **Click the Sheet1 tab**

   Sheet1, which contains the projected expenses, becomes active again. Once you have confirmed which sheet is which, you can assign them each a name that identifies their contents.

QUICK TIP

You can also rename a sheet by right-clicking the tab, clicking Rename on the shortcut menu, typing the new name, then pressing [Enter].

3. **Double-click the Sheet2 tab**

   Sheet 2 becomes the active sheet with the default sheet name of Sheet2 selected on the sheet tab.

4. **Type Actual, then press [Enter]**

   The new name automatically replaces the default name on the tab. Worksheet names can have up to 31 characters, including spaces and punctuation.

5. **Right-click the Actual tab, then click Tab Color on the shortcut menu**

   The Format Tab Color dialog box opens, as shown in Figure A-12.

QUICK TIP

To delete a worksheet, select the worksheet you want to delete, click Edit on the menu bar, then click Delete Sheet. To insert a worksheet, click Insert on the menu bar, then click Worksheet.

6. **Click the red color (first column, third row), click OK, double-click the Sheet1 tab, type Projected, then press [Enter]**

   Notice that when you renamed Sheet1, the color of the entire Actual tab changed to red. You decide to rearrange the order of the sheets, so that Actual comes before Projected.

7. **Click the Actual sheet tab and hold down the mouse button, then drag it to the left of the Projected sheet tab**

   As you drag, the pointer changes to ⌖, the sheet relocation pointer, and a small, black triangle shows its position. See Figure A-13. The first sheet in the workbook is now the Actual sheet. To see hidden sheets, click the far left tab scrolling button to display the first sheet tab; click the far right navigation button to display the last sheet tab. The left and right buttons move one sheet in their respective directions.

8. **Click the Projected sheet tab, enter your name in cell A20, then press [Ctrl][Home]**

   Your name identifies your worksheet as yours, which is helpful if you are sharing a printer.

9. **Click the Save button ⊞ on the Standard toolbar**

FIGURE A-12: Format Tab Color dialog box

Click to remove existing color from a tab

Available colors

FIGURE A-13: Moving Actual sheet before Projected sheet

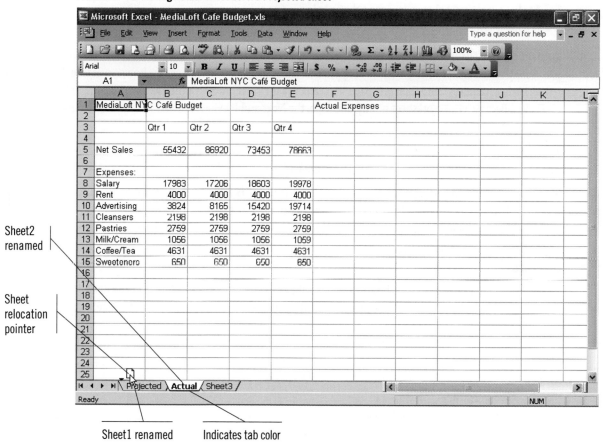

Sheet2 renamed

Sheet relocation pointer

Sheet1 renamed

Indicates tab color

Clues to Use

Copying worksheets

There are times when you may want to copy a worksheet. To copy it, press [Ctrl] as you drag the sheet tab, then release the mouse button before you release [Ctrl]. You can also move and copy worksheets between workbooks. You must have the workbook that you are copying to, as well as the workbook that you are copying from, open.

Select the sheet to copy or move, click Edit on the menu bar, then click Move or Copy sheet. Complete the information in the Move or Copy dialog box. Be sure to click the Create a copy check box if you are copying rather than moving the worksheet. Carefully check your calculation results whenever you move or copy a worksheet.

Previewing and Printing a Worksheet

After you complete a worksheet, you may want to print it to have a paper copy for reference or to give to others. You can also print a worksheet that is not complete to review your work when you are not at a computer. Before you print a worksheet, you should save any changes. That way, if anything happens to the file as it is being sent to the printer, you have your latest work saved. Then you should preview it to make sure it fits on the page the way you want. When you **preview** a worksheet, you see a copy of the worksheet exactly as it will appear on paper. See Table A-3 for a summary of printing tips. You are finished entering the labels and values into the MediaLoft budget. You have already saved your changes, so you preview the worksheet, then print a copy which you can review later.

STEPS

QUICK TIP

To print the worksheet using existing settings without previewing it, click the Print button on the Standard toolbar.

1. **Make sure the printer is on and contains paper**

   If a file is sent to print and the printer is off, an error message appears on your screen.

2. **Click the** Print Preview button **on the Standard toolbar**

   A miniature version of the worksheet appears in the Print Preview window, as shown in Figure A-14. If your worksheet requires more than one page, you can click the Next button or the Previous button to move between pages. Because your worksheet is only one page, the Next and Previous buttons are dimmed to signify they are inactive.

3. **Click** Print

   The Print dialog box opens, as shown in Figure A-15.

4. **Make sure that the** Active sheet(s) option button **is selected in the Print what section and that 1 appears in the Number of copies text box in the Copies section**

   Adjusting the value in the Number of copies text box enables you to print multiple copies. You can also print a selected range by clicking the Selection option button.

QUICK TIP

After previewing or printing a worksheet, dotted lines appear on the screen indicating individual page breaks in the printout. Page break positions vary with each printer.

5. **Click** OK

   A Printing dialog box appears briefly while the file is sent to the printer. Note that the dialog box contains a Cancel button. You can use it to cancel the print job while it is waiting in the print queue.

TABLE A-3: Worksheet printing tips

before you print	recommendation
Save the workbook	Make sure your work is saved before executing the command to print
Check the printer	Make sure that the printer is turned on and is online, that it has paper, and that there are no error messages or warning signals
Preview the worksheet	Check the formatted image for page breaks, page setup (vertical or horizontal), and overall appearance of the worksheet
Check the printer selection	Look in the Print dialog box to verify that the correct printer is selected
Check the Print what options	Look in the Print dialog box to verify that you are printing the active sheet, the entire workbook, or a range

FIGURE A-14: Print Preview window

Move to another page

Enlarge the screen image

Print the worksheet

Change print options

Zoom pointer

Return to worksheet

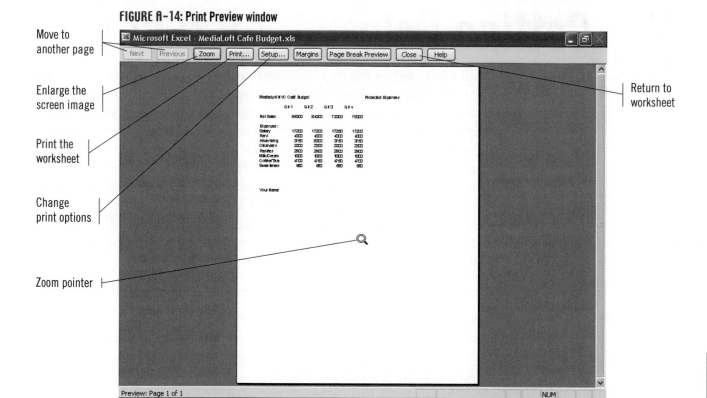

FIGURE A-15: Print dialog box

Your printer might differ

Prints the current worksheet

Indicates the number of copies to be printed

Clues to Use

Using Zoom in Print Preview

When you are in the Print Preview window, you can enlarge the image by clicking the Zoom button. You can also position the Zoom pointer ◎ over a specific part of the worksheet page, then click it to view that section of the page. Figure A-16 shows a magnified section of a document. While the image is zoomed in, use the scroll bars to view different sections of the page.

FIGURE A-16: Enlarging the preview using Zoom

Excel 2003

Getting Help

Excel features an extensive **Help system** that gives you immediate access to definitions, how to complete tasks, explanations, and useful tips. The Help task pane lets you search the Microsoft online Help database stored on the Web or the Excel Help database stored on your computer. You can type a **keyword**, a representative word on which Excel can search your area of interest, or you can access a question-and-answer format to research your Help topic. In addition, you can press [F1] at any time to display the Help task pane and get immediate assistance. Alternately, the **Type a question for help box** on the menu bar is always available for asking questions. You can click in the text box and type a question at any time to display related Help topics. Questions from your current Excel session are stored, and you can access them at any time by clicking the Type a question for help list arrow, then clicking the question of interest. ▅▅▅▅ Jim wants you to find out more about formulas so you can work more efficiently with them. He suggests you find out more information by using the Microsoft Excel Help task pane.

STEPS

QUICK TIP
You can also display the Microsoft Excel Help task pane from any open task pane. To do this, click the Other Task Panes list arrow, then click Help.

1. **Click the Microsoft Excel Help button ⓘ on the Standard toolbar**

   The Excel Help task pane opens. You can get information by typing a keyword or question in the Search text box.

2. **Type Create a formula in the Search for text box**

   See Figure A-18.

3. **Click the Start searching button →**

   Excel searches for relevant topics from the Help files and displays a list of topics from which you can choose.

4. **Click Create a formula**

   A Help window containing information about creating formulas opens, as shown in Figure A-19. Microsoft Excel Help is an online feature that by default assumes you are connected to the Internet. If you are not connected to the Internet, then your search results might differ from Figure A-19. You may have fewer search results, reflecting those topics stored locally in the Excel Help database on your computer.

QUICK TIP
Clicking the Print button 🖨 in the Help window prints the information.

5. **Read the text, then click the Close button ☒ on the Help window title bar**

   The Help window closes.

6. **Click the Close button ☒ on the Search Results task pane to close it.**

   The task pane is no longer displayed in the worksheet window.

FIGURE A-18: Help task pane

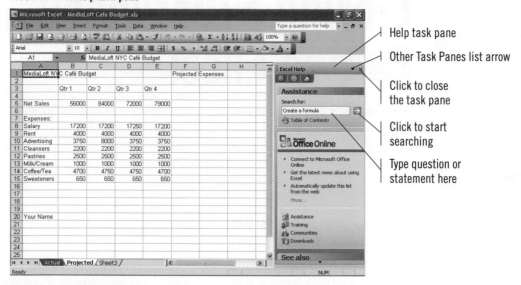

- Help task pane
- Other Task Panes list arrow
- Click to close the task pane
- Click to start searching
- Type question or statement here

FIGURE A-19: Help window

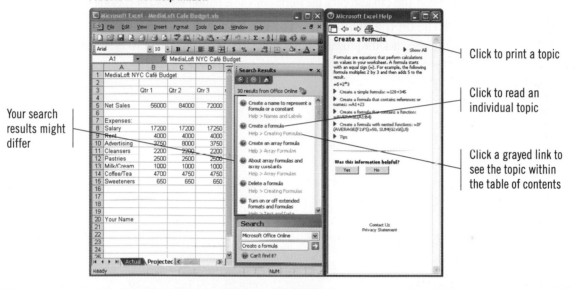

- Your search results might differ
- Click to print a topic
- Click to read an individual topic
- Click a grayed link to see the topic within the table of contents

Excel 2003

Clues to Use

Using the Office Assistant

If the Office Assistant is displayed, click it to access Help. If it is not displayed, click Help on the menu bar, then click Show the Office Assistant. (You may need to install additional components from your Microsoft Office CD in order to see the Office Assistant.) This feature provides help based on the text you type in the query box. To ask a question, click the Office Assistant. Type a question, statement, or word, as shown in Figure A-17, then click Search. The Search Results task pane searches the database and displays any matching topics. The animated Office Assistant provides Office Assistant Tips (indicated by a light bulb) on the current action you are performing. You can click the light bulb to display a dialog box containing relevant choices to which you can refer as you work. The default Office Assistant character is Clippit, but there are others from which you can choose. To change the appearance of the Office Assistant, right-click the Office Assistant, then click Options on the shortcut menu. Click the Gallery tab in the Options dialog box, click the Back and Next buttons until

you find an Assistant you want to use, then click OK. (You may need to insert your Microsoft Office CD to perform this task.)

FIGURE A-17: Office Assistant dialog box

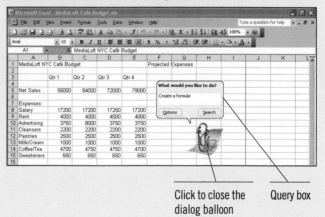

- Click to close the dialog balloon
- Query box

Closing a Workbook and Exiting Excel

When you have finished working, you need to save the workbook file and close it. When you have completed all your work in Excel you need to exit the program. You can exit Excel by clicking Exit on the File menu. ▓▓▓▓ You have completed your work on the MediaLoft budget. You want to close the workbook, then exit Excel.

1. **Click File on the menu bar**

   The File menu opens. See Figure A-20.

2. **Click Close**

   Excel closes the workbook, asking if you want to save your changes; if you have made any changes be sure to save them. You can also click the workbook Close button instead of clicking Close on the File menu.

To exit Excel and close several files at once, click Exit on the File menu. Excel prompts you to save changes to each open workbook before exiting the program.

3. **Click File on the menu bar, then click Exit**

   You can also click the program Close button to exit the program. Excel closes, and you return to the desktop.

FIGURE A-20: Closing a workbook using the File menu

Program control menu box

Workbook control menu box

Close command

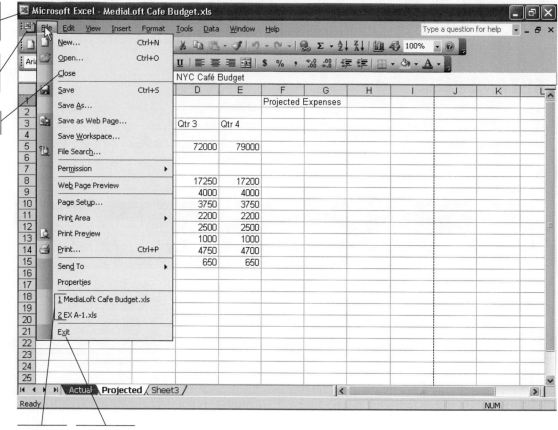

Your list might differ

Exit command

Excel 2003

Practice

▼ CONCEPTS REVIEW

Label the elements of the Excel worksheet window shown in Figure A-21.

FIGURE A-21

Match each term with the statement that best describes it.

7. **Cell**

8. **Worksheet window**

9. **Workbook**

10. **Name Box**

11. **Cell pointer**

12. **Formula bar**

a. Area that contains a grid of columns and rows

b. The intersection of a column and row

c. Allows you to enter or edit worksheet data

d. Collection of worksheets

e. Rectangle indicating the active cell

f. Displays the active cell address

Select the best answer from the list of choices.

13. **The following key(s) can be used to confirm cell entries, except:**
    a. [Enter].
    b. [Tab].
    c. [Esc].
    d. [Ctrl][Enter].

14. **Each of the following is true about labels, except:**
    a. They are left-aligned by default.
    b. They are not used in calculations.
    c. They are right-aligned by default.
    d. They can include numerical information.

15. **An electronic spreadsheet can perform all of the following tasks, except:**
    a. Display information visually.
    b. Calculate data accurately.
    c. Plan worksheet objectives.
    d. Recalculate updated information.

16. **What symbol is typed before a number to make the number a label?**
    a. '
    b. !
    c. "
    d. ;

17. **You can get Excel Help in any of the following ways, except:**
    a. Clicking Help on the menu bar, then clicking Microsoft Excel Help.
    b. Minimizing the program window.
    c. Clicking .
    d. Pressing [F1].

18. **Each of the following is true about values, except:**
    a. They can include labels.
    b. They are right-aligned by default.
    c. They are used in calculations.
    d. They can include formulas.

19. **Which button is used to preview a worksheet?**
    a.
    b.
    c.
    d.

20. **Each of the following is true about the Help feature, except:**
    a. You can use the Type a question for help text box.
    b. You can search your computer and Microsoft.com.
    c. You can change the appearance of the Office Assistant.
    d. It can complete certain tasks for you.

21. **Which feature is used to enlarge a Print Preview view?**
    a. Magnify
    b. Enlarge
    c. Amplify
    d. Zoom

▼ SKILLS REVIEW

1. **Define spreadsheet software.**
   a. Identify five disadvantages of using a nonelectronic spreadsheet.
   b. Identify five common business uses for electronic spreadsheets.

2. **Start Excel 2003.**
   a. Point to **All Programs** on the Start menu.
   b. Point to Microsoft Office, then click the **Microsoft Office Excel 2003** program icon.
   c. What appears when Excel opens?

▼ SKILLS REVIEW (CONTINUED)

3. View the Excel window.

  a. Identify as many elements in the Excel window without looking back in the unit.

  b. If the program and workbook are both maximized, which set of resizing buttons is used to minimize the workbook? (*Hint*: Would you use the upper or lower set?)

4. Open and save a workbook.

  a. Open the workbook EX A-2.xls from the drive and folder where your Data Files are located.

  b. Use the Create New Folder button in the Save As dialog box to create a folder called Toronto in the drive and folder where your Data Files are located.

  c. Save the workbook as MediaLoft Toronto Café in the Toronto folder where your Data Files are located.

  d. Close the file.

  e. Open it again from the new folder you created.

  f. Open a new workbook based on the Balance Sheet template: open the New Workbook task pane, click the On my computer link under the Templates section, display the Spreadsheet Solutions tab, then double-click Balance Sheet.

  g. Save the workbook as MediaLoft Balance Sheet in the drive and folder where your Data Files are stored, then close the workbook.

5. Enter labels and values.

  a. Enter the necessary labels shown in Table A-4. (The entry for "Water" should be in cell A4.)

  b. Enter the values shown in Table A-4.

  c. Clear the contents of cell A9 using the Edit menu, then type Tea in cell A9.

  d. Save the workbook using the Save button.

TABLE A-4

	On-Hand	Cost Each	Sale Price
Water	32	10.03	
Coffee	52	13.71	
Bread	39	15.22	
Muffins	25	16.99	
Sweets	43	11.72	
Sodas	52	9.91	

6. Name and move a sheet.

  a. Name the Sheet1 tab Inventory, then name the Sheet2 tab Sales.

  b. Move the Inventory sheet so it comes after the Sales sheet.

  c. Change the tab color of the Inventory sheet to yellow (third column, fourth row in the pallette).

  d. Change the tab color of the Sales sheet to aqua (fifth column, fourth row in the pallette).

7. Preview and print a worksheet.

  a. Make the Inventory sheet active.

  b. View it in Print Preview.

  c. Use the Zoom button to get a better look at your worksheet.

  d. Add your name to cell A11, then print one copy of the worksheet.

  e. Save the workbook.

8. Get Help.

  a. Display the Help task pane.

  b. Ask for information about defining a range.

  c. Print the information offered by the Help task pane using the Print button in the Help window.

  d. Close the Help window and task pane.

9. Close a workbook and exit Excel.

  a. Close the file using the Close command.

  b. Exit Excel.

▼ INDEPENDENT CHALLENGE 1

The Excel Help feature provides definitions, explanations, procedures, and other helpful information. It also provides examples and demonstrations to show you how Excel features work. Topics include elements such as the active cell, status bar, buttons, and dialog boxes, as well as detailed information about Excel commands and options.

    a. Start Excel and open a blank workbook using the Getting Started task pane.

    b. Display the Help task pane.

    c. Find information about displaying toolbar buttons.

Advanced Challenge Exercise

    ■ Display the Office Assistant, if necessary, using the Show Office Assistant command on the Help menu.

    ■ Click the Office Assistant, then type a question about saving a workbook in another file format. (*Hint*: You may have to ask the Office Assistant more than one question.)

    d. Print the information, close the Help window, then exit Excel.

▼ INDEPENDENT CHALLENGE 2

Spreadsheet software has many uses that can affect the way people work. The beginning of this unit discusses some examples of people using Excel. Use your own personal or business experiences to come up with five examples of how Excel can be used in a business setting.

    a. Start Excel.

    b. Write down five business tasks that you can complete more efficiently by using an Excel worksheet.

    c. Sketch a sample of each worksheet. See Table A-5, a sample payroll worksheet, as a guide.

    d. Open a new workbook and save it as **Sample Payroll** in the drive and folder where your Data Files are stored.

    e. Give your worksheet a title in cell A1, then type your name in cell D1.

    f. Enter the labels shown in Table A-5. Enter Hours Worked in column C and Hourly Wage in column E.

    g. Create and enter your own sample data for Hours Worked and Hourly Wage in the worksheet. (The entry for "Dale Havorford" should be in cell A4.)

    h. Save your work, then preview and print the worksheet.

    i. Close the worksheet and exit Excel.

TABLE A-5

Employee Name	Hours Worked	Hourly Wage
Dale Havorford		
Chris Wong		
Sharon Martinez		
Belinda Swanson		
Total		

▼ INDEPENDENT CHALLENGE 3

You are the office manager for Christine's Car Parts, a small auto parts supplier. Although the company is just three years old, it is expanding rapidly, and you are continually looking for ways to make your job easier. Last year, you began using Excel to manage and maintain data on inventory and sales, which has greatly helped you to track information accurately and efficiently. The owner of the company has just approved your request to hire an assistant, who will be starting work in a week. You want to create a short training document that acquaints your new assistant with basic Excel skills.

    a. Start Excel.

    b. Create a new workbook and save it as **Training Workbook** in the drive and folder where your Data Files are located.

    c. Model your worksheet after the sample shown in Figure A-22. Enter a title for the worksheet in cell A1.

    d. Enter your name in cell D1.

    e. Create and enter values and labels for a sample spreadsheet. Make sure you have labels in column A.

    f. Change the name of Sheet1 to Sample Data, then change the tab color of the Sample Data worksheet to another color.

    g. Preview the worksheet, then print it.

Advanced Challenge Exercise

    ■ Open a workbook based on a template from the Spreadsheet Solutions tab in the Templates dialog box. (You may need to insert your Office CD in order to do this.)

    ■ Preview the worksheet, then print it.

    ■ Save the workbook as **Template Sample**.

    h. Close the file(s) and exit Excel.

FIGURE A-22

▼ INDEPENDENT CHALLENGE 4

You can use the World Wide Web to help make informed purchasing decisions. Your supervisor has just given you approval for buying a new computer. While cost is not a limiting factor, you do need to provide a list of hardware and software requirements. You can use data found on the World Wide Web, and use Excel to create a worksheet that details your purchase decision.

a. Connect to the Internet, then use your favorite search engine to find your own information sources on computer hardware and software you can purchase.

b. Locate data for the type of system you want by using at least two different vendor's Web sites. When you find systems that meet your needs, print out the information. Be sure to identify each system's key features, such as the processor chip, hard drive capacity, RAM, and monitor size.

c. When you are finished gathering data, disconnect from the Internet.

d. Start Excel, open a new workbook, then save it in the drive and folder where your Data Files are stored as **New Computer Data**.

e. Enter the manufacturers' names in columns and computer features (RAM, etc.) in rows. List the systems you found through your research, including the features you want (e.g., CD-ROM drive, etc.) and the cost for each system.

f. Indicate on the worksheet your final purchase decision by including descriptive text in a prominent cell. Enter your name in one of the cells.

g. Save, preview, then print your worksheet.

h. Close the file and exit Excel.

▼ VISUAL WORKSHOP

Create a worksheet similar to Figure A-23 using the skills you learned in this unit. Save the workbook as **Carrie's Camera and Darkroom** in the drive and folder where your Data Files are stored. Type your name in cell A11, then preview and print the worksheet.

FIGURE A-23

Building and Editing Worksheets

OBJECTIVES

Plan and design a worksheet
Edit cell entries
Enter formulas
Create complex formulas
Introduce Excel functions
Use Excel functions
Copy and move cell entries
Understand relative and absolute cell references
Copy formulas with relative cell references
Copy formulas with absolute cell references

If you have a SAM user profile, you may have access to hands-on instruction, practice, and assessment of the skills covered in this unit. Log in to your SAM account and go to your assignments page to see what your instructor has assigned.

Using your understanding of Excel basics, you can now plan and build your own worksheets. When you build a worksheet, you enter labels, values, and formulas into worksheet cells. Once you create a worksheet, you can save it in a workbook file and then print it. ▓▓▓▓ The MediaLoft Marketing Department has asked Jim Fernandez for an estimate of the average number of author appearances this summer. Marketing hopes that the number of appearances will increase 20% over last year's figures. Jim asks you to create a worksheet that summarizes appearances for last year and forecasts the summer appearances for this year.

Planning and Designing a Worksheet

Before you start entering data into a worksheet, you need to know the purpose and approximate layout of the worksheet. ███████ To increase store traffic and sales, MediaLoft encourages authors to come to stores and sign their books. Jim wants to forecast MediaLoft's 2006 summer author appearances. The goal, already identified by the Marketing Department, is to increase the year 2005 signings by 20%. Using the planning guidelines below, Jim works with you to plan this worksheet and create it in Excel.

DETAILS

In planning and designing a worksheet it is important to:

- **Determine the purpose of the worksheet and give it a meaningful title**

  You need to forecast summer appearances for 2006. Jim suggests you title the worksheet "Summer 2006 MediaLoft Author Events Forecast."

- **Determine your worksheet's desired results, or output**

  Jim needs to begin scheduling author events and will use these forecasts to determine staffing and budget needs if the number of author events increases by 20%. He also wants to calculate the average number of author events because the Marketing Department uses this information for corporate promotions.

- **Collect all the information, or input, that will produce the results you want**

  Jim helps you by gathering together the number of author events that occurred at four stores during the 2005 summer season, which runs from June through August.

- **Determine the calculations, or formulas, necessary to achieve the desired results**

  Jim states you will first need to total the number of events at each of the selected stores during each month of the summer of 2005. Then you will need to add these totals together to determine the grand total of summer appearances. Because you need to determine the goal for the 2006 season, the 2005 monthly totals and grand total are multiplied by 1.2 to calculate the projected 20% increase for the 2006 summer season. Jim suggests you use the Average function to determine the average number of author appearances for the Marketing Department.

- **Sketch on paper how you want the worksheet to look; identify where to place the labels and values**

  Jim suggests you put the store locations in rows and the months in columns. Jim creates a sketch, in which he enters the data and notes the location of the monthly totals and the grand total. Below the totals, he writes out the formula for determining a 20% increase in 2005 appearances. He also includes a label for the calculations of the average number of events. Jim's sketch of this worksheet is shown in Figure B-1.

- **Create the worksheet**

  Jim begins creating the worksheet for you, by entering the labels first, to establish the structure of the worksheet. He then enters the values—the data summarizing the events—into the worksheet. Finally, he enters the formulas necessary to calculate totals, averages, and forecasts. These values and formulas will be used to calculate the necessary output. The worksheet Jim creates is shown in Figure B-2.

FIGURE B-1: Worksheet sketch showing labels, values, and calculations

Summer 2006 MediaLoft Author Events Forecast

	June	July	August	Total	Average
Boston	23	15	19		
New York	28	18	22		
Seattle	20	16	12		
San Diego	15	26	21		
Total	June Total	July Total	August Total	Grand Total	
20% rise	Total X 1.2				

FIGURE B-2: Forecasting worksheet

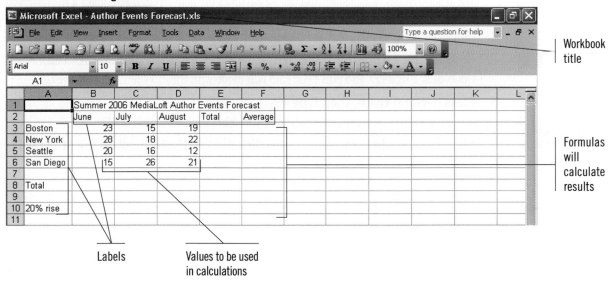

BUILDING AND EDITING WORKSHEETS **EXCEL B-3**

Excel 2003

Editing Cell Entries

You can change the contents of a cell at any time. To edit the contents of a cell, you first select the cell you want to edit. Then you have two options: you can click the formula bar or press [F2]. This puts Excel into Edit mode. Alternately, you can double-click any cell and start editing. To make sure you are in Edit mode, look at the **mode indicator** on the far left of the status bar. ▒▒▒▒▒ After planning and creating the work-sheet with Jim, you notice that he entered the wrong value for the August Seattle events, and that Houston should replace San Diego. You can edit these entries to correct them.

STEPS

1. **Start Excel, open the file** EX B-1.xls **from the drive and folder where your Data Files are stored, then save it as** Author Events Forecast

2. **Click cell** D5, **then click to the right of** 12 **in the formula bar**

   This cell contains August events for the Seattle store, which you want to change to reflect the correct num-bers. Excel goes into Edit mode, and the mode indicator on the status bar displays "Edit." A blinking vertical line called the **insertion point** appears in the formula bar, and if you move the mouse pointer to the for-mula bar, the pointer changes to I, which is used for editing. See Figure B-3.

3. **Press** [Backspace], **type** 8, **then click the** Enter button ☑ **on the formula bar**

   The value in cell D5 is changed from 12 to 18, and cell D5 remains selected.

4. **Click cell** A6, **then press** [F2]

   Excel returns to Edit mode, and the insertion point appears in the cell.

5. **Press and hold** [Shift], **press** [Home], **then release** [Shift]

   The contents of the cell is selected, and the next typed character will replace the selection.

6. **Type** Houston, **then press** [Enter]

   The label changes to Houston, and cell A7 becomes the active cell. If you make a mistake, you can click the Cancel button ☒ on the formula bar *before* confirming the cell entry. If you notice the mistake *after* you have confirmed the cell entry, click the Undo button ↺ on the Standard toolbar.

7. **Position the ⊕ pointer to the left of** 26 **in cell C6, then double-click cell** C6

   Double-clicking a cell also puts Excel into Edit mode with the insertion. point in the cell.

8. **Press** [Delete] **twice, then type** 19

   The number of book signings for July in Houston has been corrected. See Figure B-4.

9. **Click ☑ to confirm the entry, then click the** Save button 🖫 **on the Standard toolbar**

FIGURE B-3: Worksheet in Edit mode

Pointer used for editing

Insertion point in formula bar

Edit mode indicator

FIGURE B-4: Edited worksheet

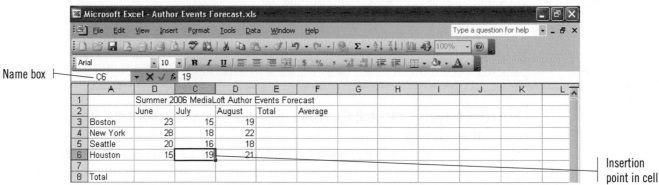

Name box

Insertion point in cell

Clues to Use

Recovering a lost workbook file

Sometimes while you are using Excel, you may experience a power failure or your computer may "freeze," making it impossible to continue working. If this type of interruption occurs, Excel has a built-in recovery feature that allows you to open and save files that were open at the time of the interruption. When you restart Excel after an interruption, the Document Recovery task pane opens on the left side of your screen displaying both original and recovered versions of the files that were open. If you're not sure which file to open (original or recovered), it's usually better to open the recovered file because it will have retained the latest information. You can, however, open and review all the versions of the file that were recovered and save the best one. Each file listed in the Document Recovery task pane has a list arrow with options that allow you to open the file, save the file, delete the file, or show repairs made to the file.

Entering Formulas

You use **formulas** to perform numeric calculations such as adding, multiplying, and averaging. Formulas in an Excel worksheet usually start with the equal sign (=), called the **formula prefix**, followed by cell addresses and range names. Arithmetic formulas use one or more **arithmetic operators** to perform calculations; see Table B-1 for a list of common arithmetic operators. Using a cell address or range name in a formula is called **cell referencing**. If you change a value in a cell, any formula containing that cell reference will be automatically recalculated using the new value. ▓▓▓▓ You need to total the values for the monthly author events for June, July, and August. You create formulas to perform these calculations.

STEPS

1. **Click cell B8**

   This is the cell where you want to enter the calculation that totals the number of June events.

2. **Type = (the equal sign)**

   Placing an equal sign at the beginning of an entry tells Excel that a formula is about to be entered, rather than a label or a value. "Enter" appears in the status bar. The total number of June events is equal to the sum of the values in cells B3, B4, B5, and B6.

   > **TROUBLE**
   > If you type an incorrect character, press [Backspace], then type the correct character.

3. **Type b3+b4+b5+b6**

   Compare your worksheet to Figure B-5. Each cell address in the equation is shown in a matching color in the worksheet. For example, the cell address B3 is written in blue in the equation and is outlined in blue in the worksheet. This makes it easy to identify each cell in a formula.

   > **TROUBLE**
   > If the formula instead of the result appears in the cell after you click ✓, make sure you began the formula with = (the equal sign).

4. **Click the Enter button ✓ on the formula bar**

   The result, 86, appears in cell B8. Cell B8 remains selected, and the formula appears in the formula bar. Excel is not case sensitive: it doesn't matter if you type uppercase or lowercase characters when you enter cell addresses. Typing cell addresses is only one way of creating a formula. A more accurate method involves **pointing** at cells using the mouse, then using the keyboard to supply arithmetic operators.

5. **Click cell C8, type =, click cell C3, type +, click cell C4, type +, click cell C5, type +, click cell C6, then click ✓**

   When you clicked cell C3, a moving border surrounded the cell. This **moving border** indicates the cell used in the calculation. Moving borders can appear around a single cell or a range of cells. The total number of author appearances for July is 68 and appears in cell C8. The pointing method of creating a formula is more accurate than typing, because it is easy to type a cell address incorrectly. You also need to enter a total for the August events in cell D8.

6. **Click cell D8, type =, click cell D3, type +, click cell D4, type +, click cell D5, type +, click cell D6, then click ✓**

   The total number of appearances for August is 80 and appears in cell D8. Compare your worksheet to Figure B-6.

7. **Click the Save button 🖫 on the Standard toolbar**

FIGURE B-5: Worksheet showing cells in a formula

Formula displayed in formula bar

Formula displayed in cell

FIGURE B-6: Completed formulas

TABLE B-1: Excel arithmetic operators

operator	purpose	example
+	Addition	=A5+A7
–	Subtraction or negation	=A5–10
*	Multiplication	=A5*A7
/	Division	=A5/A7
%	Percent	=35%
^ (caret)	Exponent	=6^2 (same as 6^2)

Creating Complex Formulas

The formula you entered is a simple formula containing one arithmetic operator, the plus sign. You can create a **complex formula**—an equation that uses more than one type of arithmetic operator. For example, you may need to create a formula that uses addition and multiplication. You can use arithmetic operators to separate tasks within a complex equation. In formulas containing more than one arithmetic operator, Excel uses the order of precedence rules to determine which operation to perform first. ⬛⬛⬛⬛ You want to total the values for the monthly author events for June, July, and August, and forecast what the 20% increase in appearances will be. You can create a complex formula to perform these calculations.

STEPS

1. **Click cell B10, type =, click cell B8, then type *.2**
   This part of the formula calculates 20% of the cell contents by multiplying the June total by .2 (or 20%). Because this part of the formula uses multiplication, it is calculated first according to the rules of precedence.

2. **Type +, then click cell B8**
   The second part of the formula adds the 20% increase to the original value of the cell. The mode indicator says Point, indicating you can add more cell references. Compare your worksheet to Figure B-7.

3. **Click the Enter button ☑ on the formula bar**
   The result, 103.2, appears in cell B10.

4. **Click cell C10, type =, click cell C8, type *.2, type +, click cell C8, then click ☑**
   The result, 81.6, appears in cell C10.

5. **Click cell D10, type =, click cell D8, type *.2, type +, click D8, then click ☑**
   The result, 96, appears in cell D10. Compare your completed worksheet to Figure B-8.

6. **Click the Save button 🖫 on the Standard toolbar**

Clues to Use

Order of precedence in Excel formulas

A formula can include several mathematical operations. When you work with formulas that have more than one operator, the order of precedence is very important. If a formula contains two or more operators, such as 4+.55/4000*25, the computer performs the calculations in a particular sequence based on these rules: Operations inside parentheses are calculated before any other operations. Exponents are calculated next, then any multiplication and division—from left to right. Finally, addition and subtraction are calculated from left to right. In the example 4+.55/4000*25, Excel performs the arithmetic operations by first dividing 4000 into .55, then multiplying the result by 25, then adding 4. You can change the order of calculations by using parentheses. For example, in the formula (4+.55)/4000*25, Excel would first add 4 and .55, then divide that amount by 4000, then finally multiply by 25.

FIGURE B-7: Elements of a complex formula

Mode indicator — Point

FIGURE B-8: Multiple complex formulas

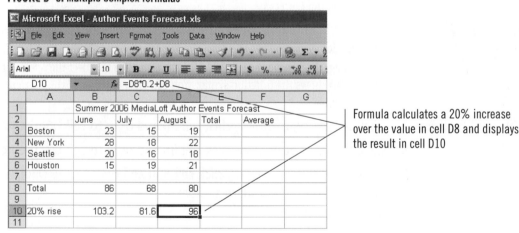

Formula calculates a 20% increase over the value in cell D8 and displays the result in cell D10

Clues to Use

Editing formulas

You edit formulas the same way you edit cell entries: you click the cell containing the formula then edit it in the formula bar; you can also double-click a cell or press [F2] to enter Edit mode, and then edit the formula in the cell. After you are in Edit mode, use the arrow keys to move the insertion point left or right in the formula. Use [Backspace] or [Delete] to delete characters to the left or right of the insertion point, then type or point to new cell references or operators.

Excel 2003

Introducing Excel Functions

Functions are predefined worksheet formulas that enable you to perform complex calculations easily. Like formulas, functions always begin with the formula prefix = (the equal sign). You can type functions, or you can use the Insert Function button on the formula bar to select the function you need from a dialog box. The **AutoSum button** on the Standard toolbar enters the most frequently used function, SUM. A function can be used by itself within a cell, or as part of a formula. For example, to calculate monthly sales tax, you could create a formula that adds a range of cells (using the SUM function) and then multiplies the total by a decimal. You use the SUM function to calculate the grand totals in the worksheet.

STEPS

1. **Click cell E3**

   This is where you want the total of all Boston author events for June, July, and August to appear.

   > **QUICK TIP**
   > The AutoSum list arrow displays commonly used functions, as well as the More Functions command that opens the Insert Function dialog box.

2. **Click the AutoSum button Σ on the Standard toolbar**

   The formula =SUM(B3:D3) appears in the formula bar and a moving border surrounds cells in the worksheet, as shown in Figure B-9.

3. **Click the Enter button ✓ on the formula bar**

   The result, 57, appears in cell E3. By default, AutoSum adds the values in the cells above the cell pointer. If there are one or fewer values there, AutoSum adds the values to its left—in this case, the values in cells B3, C3, and D3. The information inside the parentheses is the **argument**, or the information Excel uses to calculate the function result. In this case, the argument is the range B3:D3.

4. **Click cell E4, click Σ, then click ✓**

   The total for the New York events, 68, appears in cell E4.

5. **Click cell E5, then click Σ**

   AutoSum sets up a function to add the two values in the cells above the active cell, but this time the default argument is not correct.

   > **QUICK TIP**
   > The ScreenTip 1R × 3C tells you the size of the range is 1 row and 3 columns.

6. **Click cell B5 and hold down the mouse button, drag to cell D5 to select the range B5:D5, then click ✓**

   As you drag, the argument in the SUM function changes to reflect the selected range, and a yellow **Argument ScreenTip** shows the function syntax. You can click any part of the Argument ScreenTip to display Help on the function.

   > **QUICK TIP**
   > Excel automatically enters the final ")".

7. **Click cell E6, type =SUM(, click cell B6 and drag to cell D6, then click ✓**

8. **Click cell E8, type =SUM(, click cell B8 and drag to cell D8, then click ✓**

9. **Click cell E10, type =SUM(, click cell B10 and drag to cell D10, click ✓, then click the Save button 🖫 on the Standard toolbar**

   Compare your screen to Figure B-10.

FIGURE B-9: Formula and moving border

AutoSum button

SUM function in formula bar

Moving border

FIGURE B-10: Worksheet with SUM functions entered

AutoSum list arrow

Insert Function button

Result of SUM function

Clues to Use

Using the MIN and MAX functions

Other commonly used functions include MIN and MAX. You use the MIN function to calculate the minimum, or smallest, value in a selected range; the MAX function calculates the maximum, or largest, value in a selected range. The MAX function is included in the Most Recently Used function category in the Insert Function dialog box, while both the MIN and MAX function can be found in the Statistical category. These functions are particularly useful in larger worksheets and can be selected using the Insert Function button on the formula bar or the AutoSum list arrow on the Standard toolbar.

Using Excel Functions

Functions can be typed directly from the keyboard, or by using the Insert Function button on the formula bar. Clicking this button opens the Insert Function dialog box, which provides a guided method of choosing a function, describes what each function does, and helps you choose which cells to select to complete each equation. ▰▰▰▰▰ You need to use the AVERAGE function to calculate the average number of author events per store.

STEPS

TROUBLE
If the Office Assistant opens, click No, don't provide help now.

1. **Click cell F3, then click the Insert Function button f_x on the formula bar**

   The Insert Function dialog box opens, as shown in Figure B-11. Here you can select a function from a list. See Table B-2 for frequently used functions. The function you need to calculate averages—named AVERAGE—appears in the Most Recently Used function category.

2. **Click AVERAGE in the Select a function list box, then click OK**

   The Function Arguments dialog box opens.

QUICK TIP
Modify a function's range by clicking the Collapse Dialog Box button, defining the range with your mouse, then clicking the Expand Dialog Box button to return to the Function Arguments dialog box.

3. **Type B3:D3 in the Number 1 text box, as shown in Figure B-12, then click OK**

   The value 19 appears in cell F3.

4. **Click cell F4, click f_x to open the Insert Function dialog box, verify that AVERAGE is selected in the Select a function list, click OK, type B4:D4, then click OK**

5. **Click cell F5, click f_x, click AVERAGE if necessary, click OK, type B5:D5, then click OK**

6. **Click cell F6, click f_x, click AVERAGE if necessary, click OK, type B6:D6, then click OK**

   The result for Boston (cell F3) is 19; the result for New York (cell F4) is 22.66667; the result for Seattle (cell F5) is 18; and the result for Houston (cell F6) is 18.33333, giving you the averages for all four stores. See Figure B-13.

7. **Enter your name in cell A25, then click the Save button 🖫 on the Standard toolbar**

8. **Click the Print button 🖨 on the Standard toolbar**

TABLE B-2: Frequently used functions

function	description
SUM (argument)	Calculates the sum of the arguments
AVERAGE (argument)	Calculates the average of the arguments
MAX (argument)	Displays the largest value among the arguments
MIN (argument)	Displays the smallest value among the arguments
COUNT (argument)	Calculates the number of values in the arguments
PMT (rate, number of payments, loan amount)	Calculates loan payment amounts
IF (condition, if true, if false)	Determines a value if a condition is true or false
TODAY ()	Returns the current date using a date format

FIGURE B-11: Insert Function dialog box

Your list might be
ordered differently

Description of
selected function is
displayed here

FIGURE B-12: Function Arguments dialog box

Argument is
displayed here

Click the Collapse
Dialog Box button to
define an argument
using the mouse

Formula result is
displayed here

FIGURE B-13: Completed functions

Excel 2003

Copying and Moving Cell Entries

You can copy or move information from one cell or range in your worksheet to another using either the Cut, Copy, and Paste buttons, or the Excel drag-and-drop feature. When you cut or move information, the original data does not remain in the original location. You can also cut, copy, and paste labels and values from one worksheet to another. ▄▄▄▄▄▄ You need to include the 2006 forecast for spring and fall author events. Jim has already entered the spring data in the second worksheet in the workbook, and asks you to finish entering the labels and data for the fall. You copy information from the spring report to the fall report.

STEPS

1. **Click the Spring-Fall sheet tab of the Author Events Forecast workbook**
   The store names in cells A6:A7 are incorrect.

2. **Click the Summer sheet tab, select the range A5:A6, then click the Copy button 📋 on the Standard toolbar**
   The selected range (A5:A6) is copied to the **Office Clipboard**, a temporary storage area that holds the selected information you copy or cut. A moving border surrounds the selected range until you press [Esc] or copy additional information to the Clipboard. The information you copied remains in the selected range.

   TROUBLE
   If the Clipboard task pane does not open, click Edit on the menu bar, then click Office Clipboard.

3. **Click the Spring-Fall sheet tab, select the range A6:A7, then click the Paste button 📋 on the Standard toolbar**

4. **Select the range A4:A9, then click 📋**
   The Clipboard task pane opens when you copy a selection to the already occupied Clipboard. You can use the Clipboard task pane to copy, cut, store, and paste up to 24 items. Each item in the pane displays its contents.

   QUICK TIP
   After you paste an item, the Paste Options button appears. If you move the pointer over it, the Paste Options list arrow appears, letting you choose whether to paste the contents with or without its formatting, or to paste only the formatting attributes.

5. **Click cell A13, click [Boston New York Seattle Houston Total] in the Clipboard task pane to paste the contents in cell A13, then click the Close button ⊠ in the task pane title bar to close it**
   The item is copied into the range A13:A18. When pasting an item from the Clipboard into the worksheet, you only need to specify the upper-left cell of the range where you want to paste the selection. The Total label in column E is missing from the fall forecast.

6. **Click cell E3, position the pointer on any edge of the cell until the pointer changes to ⭢, then press and hold down [Ctrl]**
   The pointer changes to the Copy pointer ⭢.

7. **While still pressing [Ctrl], press and hold the left mouse button, drag the cell contents to cell E12, release the mouse button, then release [Ctrl]**
   As you dragged, an outline of the cell moved with the pointer, as shown in Figure B-14, and a ScreenTip appeared tracking the current position of the item as you moved it. When you released the mouse button, the Total label appeared in cell E12. This **drag-and-drop technique** is useful for copying cell contents. You can also use drag and drop to move data to a new cell.

   TROUBLE
   When you use drag and drop to move data into occupied cells, Excel asks if you want to replace the existing cells. Click OK to replace the contents with those of the cell you are moving.

8. **Click cell C1, position the pointer on the edge of the cell until it changes to ⭢, then drag the cell contents to A1**
   You don't use [Ctrl] when moving information with drag and drop. You can easily enter the fall events data into the range B13:D16.

9. **Select the range B13:D16, then using the information shown in Figure B-15, enter the author events data for the fall into this range, then click the Save button 💾 on the Standard toolbar**
   The **AutoCalculate** area in the status bar displays "Sum=245," which is the sum of the values in the selected range.

FIGURE B-14: Using drag and drop to copy information

Copy button

Paste button

Copied cell

Outline of copied cell

Drag-and-drop pointer with ScreenTip

FIGURE B-15: Worksheet with fall author event data entered

AutoCalculate displays sum of selected range

Clues to Use

Using the Office Clipboard

The Office Clipboard, shown in the task pane in Figure B-16, lets you copy and paste multiple items such as text, images, tables, or Excel ranges within or between Microsoft Office applications. The Office Clipboard can hold up to 24 items copied or cut from any Office or Windows-compatible program. The Clipboard task pane displays the items stored on the Office Clipboard. You choose whether to delete the first item from the Clipboard when you copy the 25th item. The collected items remain on the Office Clipboard and are available to you until you close all open Office programs. You can specify when and where to show the Office Clipboard task pane by clicking the Options list arrow at the bottom of the Clipboard task pane.

FIGURE B-16: Office Clipboard task pane

Clipboard entry from another program

Excel 2003

Understanding Relative and Absolute Cell References

As you work in Excel, you will often want to reuse formulas in different parts of the worksheet. This will save you time because you won't have to retype them. For example, you may want to perform a what-if analysis showing one set of sales figures using a lower forecast in one part of the worksheet and another set using a higher forecast in another area. But when you copy formulas, it is important to make sure that they refer to the correct cells. To do this, you need to understand relative and absolute cell references. ▰▰▰▰ Jim often reuses formulas in different parts of his worksheets to examine different possible outcomes, so he wants you to understand relative and absolute cell references.

DETAILS

- **Use relative references when cell relationships remain unchanged**

  When you create a formula that references other cells, Excel normally does not "record" the exact cell references, but instead the relationship to the cell containing the formula. For example, in Figure B-17, cell E5 contains the formula: =SUM(B5:D5). When Excel retrieves values to calculate the formula in cell E5, it actually looks for "the cell three columns to the left of the formula, which in this case is cell B5," "the cell two columns to the left of the formula," and so on. This way, if you copy the cell to a new location such as cell E6, the results will reflect the new formula location, and will automatically retrieve the values in cells B6, C6, and D6. This is called **relative cell referencing**, because Excel is recording the input cells *in relation to* the formula cell.

  In most cases, you will use relative cell references, which is the Excel default. In Figure B-17, the formulas in E5:E9 and in B9:E9 contain relative cell references. They total the "three cells to the left of" or the "four cells above" the formulas.

- **Use absolute cell references when one relationship changes**

  There are times when you want Excel to retrieve formula information from a specific cell, and you don't want that cell to change when you copy the formula to a new location. For example, you might have a price in a specific cell that you want to use in all formulas, regardless of their location. If you used relative cell referencing, the formula results would be incorrect, because Excel would use a different cell every time you copied the formula. Therefore you need to use an **absolute cell reference**, a reference that does not change when you copy the formula.

  You create an absolute cell reference by placing a $ (dollar sign) before both the column letter and the row number for the cell's address, using the [F4] function key on the keyboard. Figure B-18 displays the formulas used in Figure B-17. The formulas in cells B15 to D18 use absolute cell references to refer to a potential sales increase of 50%, shown in cell B12.

Clues to Use

Using a mixed reference

Sometimes when you copy a formula, you'll want to change the row reference, but keep the column reference the same. This type of cell referencing combines elements of both absolute and relative referencing and is called a **mixed reference**. When copied, the mixed reference C$14 changes the column relative to its new location, but prevents the row from changing. In the mixed reference $C14, the column would not change, but the row would be updated relative to its location. Like the absolute reference, a mixed reference can be created using the [F4] function key. With each press of the [F4] key, you cycle through all the possible combinations of relative, absolute, and mixed references ($C$14, C$14, $C14, C14).

FIGURE B-17: Location of relative references

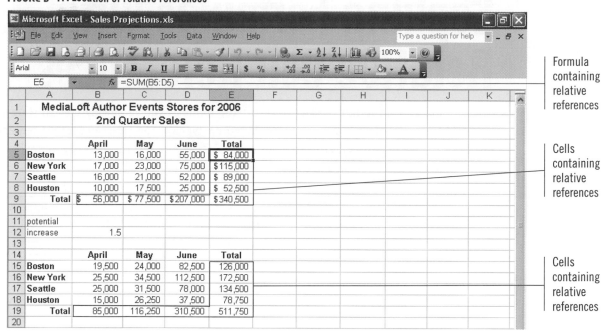

Formula containing relative references

Cells containing relative references

Cells containing relative references

FIGURE B-18: Absolute and relative reference formulas

Cell referenced in absolute formulas

Relative reference

Absolute reference

Excel 2003

Clues to Use

Printing worksheet formulas

As you create a worksheet, you may find it valuable to print the sheet showing the formulas rather than the cell contents. You can do this by clicking Tools on the menu bar, clicking Options, then clicking the View tab in the Options dialog box. Make sure a check is displayed in the Formulas check box, then click OK. When the Options dialog box closes, the cells are expanded to display the formulas, as shown in Figure B-18, and you can print the worksheet. To return the worksheet to its normal appearance, reopen the Options dialog box and deselect the Formulas check box.

Copying Formulas with Relative Cell References

Copying and moving formulas allows you to reuse formulas you've already created. Copying formulas, rather than retyping them, is faster and helps to prevent typing errors. You can use the Copy and Paste commands or the Fill Right method to copy formulas. ░░░░░ You want to copy the formulas that total the author appearances by region and by month from the spring to the fall.

STEPS

1. **Click cell E4, then click the Copy button 🖻 on the Standard toolbar**

   The formula for calculating the total number of spring Boston author events is copied to the Clipboard. Notice that the formula =SUM(B4:D4) appears in the formula bar.

2. **Click cell E13, then click the Paste button 🖺 on the Standard toolbar**

   The formula from cell E4 is copied into cell E13, where the new result of 59 appears. Notice in the formula bar that the cell references have changed, so that the range B13:D13 appears in the formula. This formula contains relative cell references, which tell Excel to copy the formula to a new cell, but to substitute new cell references so that the relationship of the cells to the formula in its new location remains unchanged. In this case, Excel adjusted the formula so that cells D13, C13, and B13—the three cell references immediately to the left of E13—replaced cells D4, C4, and B4, the three cell references to the left of E4. Notice that the lower-right corner of the active cell contains a small square, called the **fill handle**. You can use the fill handle to copy labels, formulas, and values. This option is called **AutoFill**.

3. **Position the pointer over the fill handle until it changes to ✛, press and hold the left mouse button, then drag the fill handle to select the range E13:E16**

   See Figure B-19.

4. **Release the mouse button**

   A formula similar to the one in cell E13 now appears in the range E14:E16. Again, because the formula uses relative cell references, cells E14 through E16 correctly display the totals for the fall author events. After you release the mouse button, the **AutoFill Options button** appears. If you move the pointer over it and click its list arrow, you can specify what you want to fill and whether or not you want to include formatting.

5. **Click cell B9, click Edit on the menu bar, then click Copy**

6. **Click cell B18, click Edit on the menu bar, then click Paste**

   See Figure B-20. The formula for calculating the September events appears in the formula bar. You also need totals to appear in cells C18, D18, and E18. You could use the fill handle again, but another option is the Fill command on the Edit menu.

7. **Select the range B18:E18**

8. **Click Edit on the menu bar, point to Fill, then click Right**

   The rest of the totals are filled in correctly. Compare your worksheet to Figure B-21.

9. **Click the Save button 🖫 on the Standard toolbar**

QUICK TIP

To specify components of the copied cell or range prior to pasting, click Edit on the menu bar, then click Paste Special. You can selectively copy formulas, values, and other more complex features.

TROUBLE

If the Clipboard task pane opens, click the Close button. If the Office Assistant appears, right-click it, then click Hide.

FIGURE B-19: Selected range using the fill handle

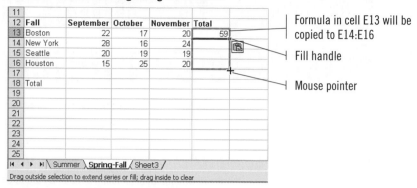

Formula in cell E13 will be copied to E14:E16

Fill handle

Mouse pointer

FIGURE B-20: Copied formula

Copied formula cell references

Paste Options button

Copied formula result

FIGURE B-21: Completed worksheet with all formulas copied

12	Fall	September	October	November	Total
13	Boston	22	17	20	59
14	New York	28	16	24	68
15	Seattle	20	19	19	58
16	Houston	15	25	20	60
17					
18	Total	85	77	83	245
19					
20					
21					
22					
23					
24					
25					

Clues to Use

Filling cells with sequential text or values

Often, you'll need to fill cells with sequential text: months of the year, days of the week, years, or text plus a number (Quarter 1, Quarter 2,...). You can easily fill cells using sequences by dragging the fill handle. As you drag the fill handle, Excel automatically extends the existing sequence. (The contents of the last filled cell appear in the ScreenTip.) Use the Fill Series command on the Edit menu to examine all of the available fill series options.

Copying Formulas with Absolute Cell References

When copying formulas, you might want a cell reference to always refer to a particular cell address. In such an instance, you would use an absolute cell reference. An absolute cell reference always refers to a specific cell address when the formula is copied. You create an absolute reference by placing a dollar sign ($) before the row letter and column number of the address (for example $A$1). ▰▰▰ The staff in the Marketing Department hopes the number of author events will increase by 20% over last year's figures. Jim asks you to add a column that calculates a possible increase in the number of spring events in 2006. You can then do a what-if analysis and recalculate the spreadsheet several times, changing the percentage by which the number of appearances might increase each time.

STEPS

1. **Click cell G1, type Change, then press [→]**
   You can store the increase factor that will be used in the what-if analysis in cell H1.

2. **Type 1.1, then press [Enter]**
   The value in cell H1 represents a 10% increase in author events.

3. **Click cell G3, type What if?, then press [Enter]**

4. **In cell G4, type =, click E4, type *, click H1, then click the Enter button ✔ on the formula bar**
   The result, 56.1, appears in cell G4. This value represents the total spring events for Boston if there is a 10% increase. Jim wants you to perform a what-if analysis for all the stores.

> **QUICK TIP**
> Before you copy or move a formula, check to see if you need to use an absolute cell reference.

5. **Drag the fill handle to extend the selection from G4 to G7**
   The resulting values in the range G5:G7 are all zeros. When you copy the formula it adjusts so that the formula in cell G5 is =E5*H2. Because there is no value in cell H2, the result is 0, an error. You need to use an absolute reference in the formula to keep the formula from adjusting itself. That way, it will always reference cell H1. You can change the relative cell reference to an absolute cell reference by using [F4].

6. **Click cell G4, press [F2] to change to Edit mode, then press [F4]**
   When you press [F2], the range finder outlines the arguments of the equation in blue and green. When you press [F4], dollar signs appear, changing the H1 cell reference to an absolute reference. See Figure B-22.

7. **Click ✔, then drag the fill handle to extend the selection to range G4:G7**
   The formula correctly contains an absolute cell reference, and the value of G4 remains unchanged at 56.1. The correct values for a 10% increase appear in cells G4:G7. You complete the what-if analysis by changing the value in cell H1 to indicate a 20% increase in events.

8. **Click cell H1, type 1.2, then click ✔**
   The values in the range G4:G7 change to reflect the 20% increase. Compare your completed worksheets to Figure B-23. Because events only occur in whole numbers, the appearance of the numbers can be changed later.

9. **Enter your name in cell A25, click the Save button 🖫 on the Standard toolbar, click the Print button 🖨 on the Standard toolbar, close the workbook, then exit Excel**

FIGURE B-22: Absolute cell reference in cell G4

Absolute cell references in formula

Incorrect values from relative referencing in copied formulas

FIGURE B-23: Completed worksheets

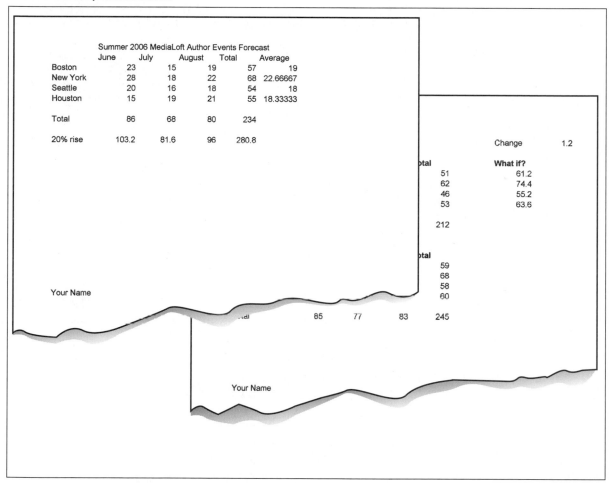

Clues to Use

Inserting and deleting selected cells

As you add formulas to your workbook, you may need to insert or delete cells, not entire rows or columns. When you do this, Excel automatically adjusts cell references to reflect their new locations. To insert cells, click Insert on the menu bar, then click Cells. The Insert dialog box opens, asking if you want to insert a cell and move the selected cell down or to the right of the new one. To delete one or more selected cells, click Edit on the menu bar, click Delete, and in the Delete dialog box, indicate which way you want to move the adjacent cells. When using this option, be careful not to disturb row or column alignment that may be necessary to make sense of the worksheet.

Practice

▼ CONCEPTS REVIEW

Label each element of the Excel worksheet window shown in Figure B-24.

FIGURE B-24

Match each term or button with the statement that best describes it.

8.

9. **Function**

10. **Formula**

11. **Fill handle**

12.

a. A predefined formula that provides a shortcut for commonly used calculations

b. A cell entry that performs a calculation in an Excel worksheet

c. Used to copy labels, formulas, and values

d. Adds the selected range to the Office Clipboard

e. Used to paste cells

Select the best answer from the list of choices.

13. **Which button is used to enter data in a cell?**

    a. ↺

    c. 📋

    b. ✖

    d ✔

14. **What type of cell reference changes when it is copied?**

    a. Circular

    c. Looping

    b. Absolute

    d. Relative

15. **What character is used to make a reference absolute?**

    a. $

    c. @

    b. ^

    d. &

▼ SKILLS REVIEW

1. **Plan and design a worksheet.**

    a. Using the scenario of tracking quarterly sales at a formal-wear rental shop, determine what sort of output would be required.

    b. Determine what kind of input would be required.

    c. What sort of formulas might be needed?

    d. Make a paper sketch of how the worksheet might look.

2. **Edit cell entries.**

    a. Start Excel, open the workbook EX B-2.xls from the drive and folder where your Data Files are stored, then save it as **Office Furnishings**.

    b. Change the quantity of Tables to **27**.

    c. Change the price of Desks to **285**.

    d. Change the quantity of Easels to **18**.

    e. Enter your name in cell A40, then save the workbook.

3. **Enter formulas.**

    a. In cell B6, use the pointing method to enter the formula **B2+B3+B4+B5**.

    b. In cell D2, enter the formula **B2*C2**.

    c. Save your work.

4. **Create complex formulas.**

    a. In cell B8, enter the formula **(B2+B3+B4+B5)/4**.

    b. In cell C8, enter the formula **(C2+C3+C4+C5)/4**.

    c. Save your work.

5. **Introduce Excel functions.**

    a. Delete the contents of cell B6.

    b. In cell B6, use the AutoSum feature to calculate the sum of B2:B5.

    c. Save your work.

6. **Use Excel functions.**

    a. Enter the label **Min Price** in cell A9.

    b. In cell C9, enter the function **MIN(C2:C5)**.

    c. Enter the label **Max Price** in cell A10.

    d. Create a formula in cell C10 that determines the maximum price of for the range C2:C5.

    e. Save your work.

7. **Copy and move cell entries.**

    a. Select the range **A1:C6**, then copy the range to cell A12.

    b. Select the range **D1:E1**, then use drag and drop to copy the range to cell D12.

    c. Move the contents of cell G1 to cell E9, then save your work.

8. **Understand relative and absolute cell references.**
   a. Write a brief description of the difference between a relative and absolute reference.
   b. Provide a sketched example of a relative and absolute reference.

9. **Copy formulas with relative cell references.**
   a. Copy the formula in D2 into cells D3:D5.
   b. Copy the formula in D2 into cells D13:D16.
   c. Save the worksheet.

10. **Copy formulas with absolute cell references.**
   a. In cell E10, enter the value **1.375**.
   b. In cell E2, create a formula containing an absolute reference that multiplies D2 and E10.
   c. Use the fill handle to copy the formula in E2 into cells **E3:E5**.
   d. Use the Copy and Paste buttons to copy the formula in E2 into cells **E13:E16**.
   e. Use the Delete command on the Edit menu to delete cells A13:E13, shifting the cells up.
   f. Change the amount in cell E10 to **3.45**.
   g. Select cells A1:E1 and insert cells, shifting cells down.
   h. Enter **Inventory Estimate** in cell A1.
   i. Save, preview, print, and close the workbook, then exit Excel.

▼ INDEPENDENT CHALLENGE 1

You are the box office manager for the Young Brazilians Jazz Band, a popular new group. Your responsibilities include tracking seasonal ticket sales for the band's concerts and anticipating ticket sales for the next season. The group sells four types of tickets: reserved, general, senior, and student tickets.

The 2006–2007 season includes five scheduled concerts: Spring, Summer, Fall, Winter, and Thaw. You will plan and build a worksheet that tracks the sales of each of the four ticket types for all five concerts.

a. Think about the results you want to see, the information you need to build into these worksheets, and what types of calculations must be performed.
b. Sketch sample worksheets on a piece of paper to indicate how the information should be laid out. What information should go in the columns? What information should go in the rows?
c. Start Excel, open a new workbook, then save it as **Young Brazilians** in the drive and folder where your Data Files are stored.
d. Plan and build a worksheet that tracks the sales of each of the four ticket types for all five concerts. Build the worksheets by entering a title, row labels, column headings, and formulas.
e. Enter your own sales data that shows that no concert sold more than 400 tickets, and the Reserved category was the most popular.
f. Calculate the total ticket sales for each concert, the total sales for each of the four ticket types, and the total sales for all tickets.
g. Name the worksheet **Sales Data** and color the worksheet tab red.
h. Copy the Sales Data worksheet to a blank worksheet, name the copied worksheet **5% Increase**, then color the sheet tab aqua.
i. Modify the 5% Increase sheet so that a 5% increase in sales of all ticket types is shown in a separate column with an appropriate column label. See Figure B-25 for a sample worksheet.
j. Enter your name in a cell in each worksheet.
k. Save your work, preview and print the worksheets, then close the workbook and exit Excel.

FIGURE B-25

	A	B	C	D	E	F	G	H	I	J	K	L
1			2006-2007 Season									
2			Young Brazilians Jazz Band					Increase				
3								1.05				
4		Reserved	General	Senior	Student							
5	Concerts	Seating	Admission	Citizens	Tickets	Totals		What if?				
6	Spring	285	50	40	20	395		414.75				
7	Summer	135	25	35	20	215		225.75				
8	Fall	130	50	25	20	225		236.25				
9	Winter	160	100	30	20	310		325.5				
10	Thaw	250	75	35	20	380		399				
11	Total	960	300	165	100	1525		1601.25				
12												

▼ INDEPENDENT CHALLENGE 2

The Beautiful You Salon is a small but growing beauty salon that has hired you to organize its accounting records using Excel. The owners want you to track the salon's expenses using Excel. Before you were hired, one of the bookkeepers entered last year's expenses in a workbook, but the analysis was never completed.

a. Start Excel, open the workbook EX B-3.xls, then save it as **Beautiful You Finances** in the drive and folder where your Data Files are stored. The worksheet includes labels for functions such as the Average, Maximum, and Minimum amounts of each of the expenses in the worksheet.

b. Think about what information would be important for the bookkeeping staff to know.

c. Create your sketch using the existing worksheet as a foundation.

d. Create formulas in the Total column and row using the AutoSum function.

e. Rename Sheet1 **Expenses** and add a color to the sheet tab.

Advanced Challenge Exercise

- Create formulas in the Average, Maximum, and Minimum columns and rows using the appropriate functions, dragging to select the range.
- Create a formula using the COUNT function that determines the total number of expense categories listed per quarter.

f. Enter your name in a worksheet cell, then compare your screen to the sample worksheet shown in Figure B-26.

g. Preview the worksheet, then print it.

h. Save the workbook, then close the workbook and exit Excel.

FIGURE B-26

	A	B	C	D	E	F	G	H	I	J	K	L
1	Beautiful You Salon											
2												
3	Operating Expenses for 2006											
4												
5	Expense	Quarter 1	Quarter 2	Quarter 3	Quarter 4	Total	Average	Maximum	Minimum			
6	Rent	4750	4750	4750	4750	19000	4750	4750	4750			
7	Utilities	8624	7982	7229	8096	31931	7982.75	8624	7229			
8	Payroll	23456	26922	25876	29415	105669	26417.25	29415	23456			
9	Insurance	8355	8194	8225	8327	33101	8275.25	8355	8194			
10	Education	4749	3081	6552	4006	18388	4597	6552	3081			
11	Inventory	29986	27115	25641	32465	115207	28801.75	32465	25641			
12	Total	79920	78044	78273	87059	323296						
13												
14	Average	13320	13007.33	13045.5	14509.83							
15	Maximum	29986	27115	25876	32465							
16	Minimum	4749	3081	4750	4006							
17	Count	6										

▼ INDEPENDENT CHALLENGE 3

You have been promoted to computer lab manager at Learn-It-All, a local computer training center. It is your responsibility to make sure there are enough computers for students during scheduled classes. Currently, you have five classrooms: four with IBM PCs and one with Macintoshes. Classes are scheduled Monday, Wednesday, and Friday in two-hour increments from 9 a.m. to 5 p.m. (the lab closes at 7 p.m.), and each room can currently accommodate 32 computers.

You plan and build a worksheet that tracks the number of students who can currently use the available computers per room. You create your enrollment data. Using an additional worksheet, you show the impact of an enrollment increase of 25%.

    a. Think about how to construct these worksheets to create the desired output.

    b. Sketch sample paper worksheets to indicate how the information should be laid out.

    c. Start Excel, open a new workbook, then save it as **Learn-it-All** in the drive and folder where your Data Files are stored.

    d. Create a worksheet by entering a title, row labels, column headings, data, and formulas. Name the sheet to easily identify its contents.

    e. Create a second sheet by copying the information from the initial sheet.

    f. Name the second sheet to easily identify its contents.

    g. Add color to each sheet tab, then compare your screen to the sample shown in Figure B-27.

    h. Enter your name in a cell in each sheet.

    i. Save your work, preview and print each worksheet, then close the workbook and exit Excel.

FIGURE B-27

	A	B	C	D	E	F	G	H	I	J
1	Computer Lab Schedule - Increased enrollment									
2										
3	Monday	PC room #1	PC room #2	PC room #3	PC room #4	Mac room #1				
4	9:00	40	40	40	40	40				
5	11:00	40	40	40	40	40				
6	1:00	40	40	40	40	40				
7	3:00	40	40	40	40	40				
8	5:00	40	40	40	40	40				
9		200	200	200	200	200				
10										
11	Wednesday	PC room #1	PC room #2	PC room #3	PC room #4	Mac room #1				
12	9:00	40	40	40	40	40				
13	11:00	40	40	40	40	40				
14	1:00	40	40	40	40	40				
15	3:00	40	40	40	40	40				
16	5:00	40	40	40	40	40				
17		200	200	200	200	200				
18										
19	Friday	PC room #1	PC room #2	PC room #3	PC room #4	Mac room #1				
20	9:00	40	40	40	40	40				
21	11:00	40	40	40	40	40				
22	1:00	40	40	40	40	40				
23	3:00	40	40	40	40	40				
24	5:00	40	40	40	40	40				
25		200	200	200	200	200				

Tabs: Actual / **Increased** / Sheet3

Ready — NUM

▼ INDEPENDENT CHALLENGE 4

Your company is opening a branch office in Great Britain and your boss is a fanatic about keeping the thermostats at a constant temperature during each season of the year. Because she grew up in the United States, she is only familiar with Fahrenheit temperatures and doesn't know how to convert them to Celsius. She has asked you to find out the Celsius equivalents for the thermostatic settings she wants to use. She prefers the temperature to be 65 degrees F in the winter, 62 degrees F in the spring, 75 degrees F in the summer, and 70 degrees F in the fall. You can use the Web and Excel to determine the new settings.

a. Start Excel, open a new workbook, then save it as **Temperature Conversions** in the drive and folder where your Data Files are stored.

b. Use your favorite search engine to find your own information sources on calculating temperature conversions.

c. Think about how to create an Excel equation that can perform the conversion.

d. Create column and row titles using Table B-3 to get started.

e. In the appropriate cell, create an equation that calculates the conversion of a Fahrenheit temperature to a Celsius temperature.

f. Copy the equation, then paste it in the remaining Celsius cells.

TABLE B-3

Temperature Conversions		
Season	Fahrenheit	Celsius
Spring	62	
Winter	65	
Summer	75	
Fall	70	

Advanced Challenge Exercise

- Copy the contents of Sheet1 to Sheet2.
- In Sheet2, change the display so the formulas are visible, then print it.

g. Enter your name in one of the cells in each sheet, preview Sheet1, then print it.

h. Save the workbook, then close the files and exit Excel.

▼ VISUAL WORKSHOP

Create a worksheet similar to Figure B-28 using the skills you learned in this unit. Save the workbook as **Annual Budget** in the drive and folder where your Data Files are stored. Enter your name in cell A13, then preview and print the worksheet.

FIGURE B-28

	A	B	C	D	E	F	G
1	Computer Consultants, Inc.						
2							
3		Hardware	Software	Training	Contracts	Total	
4	Quarter 1	86600	14200	6100	21000	127900	
5	Quarter 2	96000	16800	5000	24600	142400	
6	Quarter 3	79200	14600	9000	21000	123800	
7	Quarter 4	100600	24900	6750	30600	162850	
8	Total	362400	70500	26850	97200		
9							
10	1.7						
11	Increase	616080	119850	45645	165240		
12							
13	Your Name						

Budget / Sheet2 / Sheet3

Ready

NUM

Formatting a Worksheet

OBJECTIVES

Format values
Use fonts and font sizes
Change attributes and alignment
Adjust column widths
Insert and delete rows and columns
Apply colors, patterns, and borders
Use conditional formatting
Check spelling

If you have a SAM user profile, you may have access to hands-on instruction, practice, and assessment of the skills covered in this unit. Log in to your SAM account and go to your assignments page to see what your instructor has assigned.

You can use Excel formatting features to make a worksheet more attractive, to make it easier to read, or to emphasize key data. You do this by using different colors and fonts for the cell contents, adjusting column and row widths, and inserting and deleting columns and rows. The marketing managers at MediaLoft have asked Jim Fernandez to create a workbook that lists advertising expenses for all MediaLoft stores. Jim has prepared a worksheet for the New York City store containing this information, which he can adapt later for use in other stores. He asks you to use formatting to make the worksheet easier to read and to call attention to important data.

Formatting Values

If you enter a value in a cell and you don't like the way the data appears, you can adjust the cell's format. A cell's **format** determines how labels and values appear in it, such as boldface, italic, with or without dollar signs or commas, and the like. Formatting changes only the way a value or label appears; it does not alter cell data in any way. To format a cell, first select it, then apply the formatting. You can format cells and ranges before or after you enter data. ▓▓▓▓ The Marketing Department has requested that Jim begin by listing the New York City store's advertising expenses. Jim developed a worksheet that lists advertising invoices, entered all the information, and now he wants you to format some of the labels and values. Because some of the changes might also affect column widths, you make all formatting changes before widening the columns.

STEPS

QUICK TIP

To save a workbook in a different location, you click File on the menu bar, click Save As, click the Save in list arrow in the Save As dialog box, navigate to a new drive or folder, type a new filename if necessary, then click Save.

1. **Start Excel, open the file** EX C-1.xls **from the drive and folder where your Data Files are stored, then save it as** Ad Expenses.

   The NYC advertising worksheet appears in Figure C-1. You can display numeric data in a variety of ways, such as with decimals or leading dollar signs. Excel provides a special format for currency, which adds two decimal places and a dollar sign.

2. **Select the range** E4:E32, **then click the** Currency Style button 🔳 **on the Formatting toolbar**

   Excel adds dollar signs and two decimal places to the Cost data. Excel automatically resizes the column to display the new formatting. Another way to format dollar values is to use the comma format, which does not include the dollar sign ($).

QUICK TIP

Select any range of contiguous cells by clicking the top-left cell, pressing and holding [Shift], then clicking the bottom-right cell. Add a row to the selected range by continuing to hold down [Shift] and pressing ↓; add a column by pressing →.

3. **Select the range** G4:I32, **then click the** Comma Style button 🔳 **on the Formatting toolbar**

   The values in columns G, H, and I display the comma format. You can also format percentages by using the Formatting toolbar.

4. **Select the range** J4:J32, **click the** Percent Style button 🔳 **on the Formatting toolbar, then click the** Increase Decimal button 🔳 **on the Formatting toolbar to show one decimal place**

   The data in the % of Total column is now formatted with a percent sign (%) and one decimal place. You decide that you prefer the percentages rounded to the nearest whole number.

5. **Click the** Decrease Decimal button 🔳 **on the Formatting toolbar**

   You can also apply a variety of formats to dates in a worksheet.

6. **Select the range** B4:B31, **click** Format **on the menu bar, click** Cells, **then if necessary click the** Number tab **in the Format Cells dialog box**

   The Format Cells dialog box opens with the Date category already selected on the Number tab. See Figure C-2.

7. **Select the format** 14-Mar-01 **in the Type list box, then click** OK

   The dates in column B appear in the format you selected. You decide you don't need the year to appear in the Inv. Due column. You can quickly open the Format Cells dialog box by right-clicking a selected range.

QUICK TIP

The 3-14-01 date format displays a single-digit date (such as 5/9/06) as does 9-May-06. The date format below it displays the same date as 5/09/06.

8. **Select the range** C4:C31, **right-click the range, click** Format Cells **on the shortcut menu, click** 14-Mar **in the Type list box in the Format Cells dialog box, then click** OK

   Compare your worksheet to Figure C-3.

9. **Click the** Save button 🔳 **on the Standard toolbar**

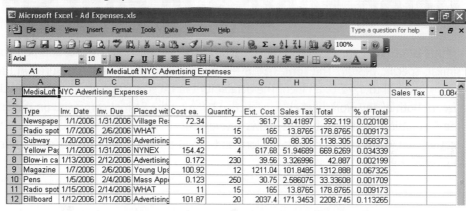

FIGURE C-1: Advertising expense worksheet

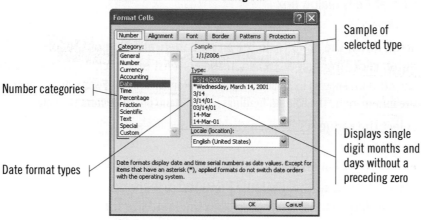

FIGURE C-2: Format Cells dialog box

Number categories

Date format types

Sample of selected type

Displays single digit months and days without a preceding zero

FIGURE C-3: Worksheet with formatted values

Dates formatted to appear without year

Clues to Use

Using the Format Painter

You can "paint" a cell's format into other cells by using the Format Painter button [img] on the Standard toolbar. This is similar to using copy and paste to copy information, but instead of copying cell contents, you copy only the cell format. Select the cell containing the desired format, then click [img]. The pointer changes to [img]. Use this pointer to select the cell or range you want to contain the new format. You can paint a cell's format into multiple cells by double-clicking [img], then clicking each cell that you want to paint with [img]. When you are finished painting formats, you can turn off the Format Painter by pressing [Esc] or by clicking [img] again.

Using Fonts and Font Sizes

A **font** is the name for a collection of characters (letters, numerals, symbols, and punctuation marks) with a similar, specific design. The **font size** is the physical size of the text, measured in units called points. A **point** is equal to 1/72 of an inch. The default font in Excel is 10-point Arial. You can change the font, the size, or both of any worksheet entry or section by using the Format command on the menu bar or by using the Formatting toolbar. Table C-1 shows several fonts in different sizes. ▓▓▓▓▓ Now that the data is formatted, Jim wants you to change the font and size of the labels and the worksheet title so that they stand out more from the data.

STEPS

1. **Press** [Ctrl][Home] **to select cell A1**

2. **Right-click cell** A1, **click** Format Cells **on the shortcut menu, then click the** Font tab **in the Format Cells dialog box**
    See Figure C-4.

3. **Scroll down the** Font list **to see an alphabetical listing of the fonts available on your computer, click** Times New Roman **in the Font list box, click** 24 **in the Size list box, then click** OK
    The title font appears in 24-point Times New Roman, and the Formatting toolbar displays the new font and size information. The column headings should stand out more from the data.

4. **Select the range** A3:J3, **then click the** Font list arrow | Arial ▾ | **on the Formatting toolbar**
    Notice that the font names on this font list are displayed in the font they represent.

5. **Click** Times New Roman **in the Font list, click the** Font Size **list arrow** | 10 ▾ | **on the Formatting toolbar, then click** 14 **in the Font Size list**
    Compare your worksheet to Figure C-5. Notice that some of the column headings are now too wide to appear fully in the column. Excel does not automatically adjust column widths to accommodate cell formatting; you have to adjust column widths manually. You'll learn to do this in a later lesson.

6. **Click the** Save button 🖫 **on the Standard toolbar**

TABLE C-1: Types of fonts

font	12 point	24 point
Arial	Excel	Excel
Playbill	Excel	Excel
Comic Sans MS	Excel	Excel
Times New Roman	Excel	Excel

FIGURE C-4: Font tab in the Format Cells dialog box

Currently selected font

Available fonts might differ on your computer

Effects options

Type a custom font size or select from the list

Font style options

Sample of selected font

FIGURE C-5: Worksheet with formatted title and labels

Font and size of active cell or range

Title appears in 24-point Times New Roman

Column headings now 14-point Times New Roman

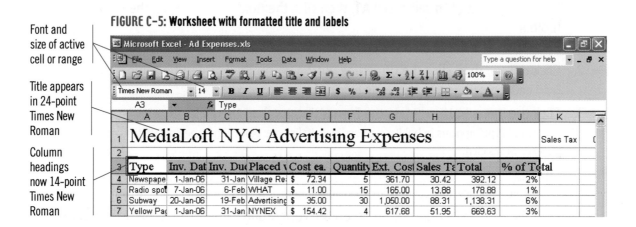

Clues to Use

Inserting and adjusting clip art

You can add clips to your worksheets to make them look more professional. A **clip** is an individual media file, such as art, sound, animation, or a movie. **Clip art** refers to images such as a corporate logo, a picture, or a photo; Excel comes with many clips that you can use. To add clip art to your worksheet, click Insert on the menu bar, point to Picture, then click Clip Art. The Insert Clip Art task pane appears. Here you can search for clips by typing one or more keywords (words related to your subject) in the Search text box, then clicking Search. Clips that relate to your keywords appear in the Clip Art task pane, as shown in Figure C-6. Click the image you want. (If you have a standard Office installation and have an active Internet connection, you will have more images available.) You can also add your own images to a worksheet by clicking Insert on the menu bar, pointing to Picture, then clicking From File. Navigate to the file you want, then click Insert. To resize an image, drag its lower-right corner. To move an image, drag it to a new location.

FIGURE C-6: Results of Clip Art search

FORMATTING A WORKSHEET EXCEL C-5

Changing Attributes and Alignment

Attributes are styling formats such as bold, italics, and underlining that you can apply to affect the way text and numbers look in a worksheet. You can also change the **alignment** of labels and values in cells to be left, right, or center. You can apply attributes and alignment options using the Formatting toolbar or using the Alignment tab of the Format Cells dialog box. See Table C-2 for a list and description of the available attribute and alignment toolbar buttons. Now that you have applied new fonts and font sizes to the worksheet labels, Jim wants you to further enhance the worksheet's appearance by adding bold and underline formatting and centering some of the labels.

STEPS

1. **Press [Ctrl][Home] to select cell A1, then click the Bold button B on the Formatting toolbar**
   The title appears in bold.

QUICK TIP

Use formatting shortcuts on any selected range: [Ctrl][B] to bold, [Ctrl][I] to italicize, and [Ctrl][U] to underline.

2. **Click cell A3, then click the Underline button U on the Formatting toolbar**
   Excel underlines the text in the column heading in the selected cell.

3. **Click the Italics button I on the Formatting toolbar, then click B**
   The word "Type" appears in boldface, underlined, italic type. Notice that the Bold, Italics, and Underline buttons are all selected.

QUICK TIP

Overuse of any attribute can be distracting and make a workbook less readable. Be consistent, adding emphasis the same way throughout.

4. **Click I**
   Excel removes italics from cell A3, but the bold and underline formatting attributes remain.

5. **Click the Format Painter button ✍ on the Formatting toolbar, then select the range B3:J3**
   Bold formatting is added to the rest of the labels in the column headings. The title would look better if it were centered over the data columns.

6. **Select the range A1:J1, then click the Merge and Center button 🔳 on the Formatting toolbar**
   The Merge and Center button creates one cell out of the 10 cells across the row, then centers the text in that newly created large cell. The title "MediaLoft NYC Advertising Expenses" is centered across the 10 columns you selected. You can change the alignment within individual cells using toolbar buttons; you can split merged cells into their original components by selecting the merged cells, then clicking 🔳.

QUICK TIP

To clear all formatting for a selected range, click Edit on the menu bar, point to Clear, then click Formats.

7. **Select the range A3:J3, then click the Center button ▤ on the Formatting toolbar**
   Compare your screen to Figure C-7. Although they may be difficult to read, notice that all the headings are centered within their cells.

8. **Click the Save button 🖫 on the Standard toolbar**

Clues to Use

Rotating and indenting cell entries

In addition to applying fonts and formatting attributes, you can rotate or indent cell data within a cell to further change its appearance. You can rotate text within a cell by altering its alignment. To change alignment, select the cells you want to modify, click Format on the menu bar, click Cells, then click the Alignment tab in the Format Cells dialog box. Click a position in the Orientation box, or type a number in the Degrees text box to change from the default horizontal alignment, then click OK. You can indent cell contents using the Increase Indent button 🔳 on the Formatting toolbar, which moves cell contents to the right one space, or the Decrease Indent button 🔳, which moves cell contents to the left one space.

FIGURE C-7: Worksheet with formatting attributes applied

Formatting
buttons
selected

Title centered
across
columns

Column
headings
centered,
bold, and
underlined

Center button

Merge and
Center button

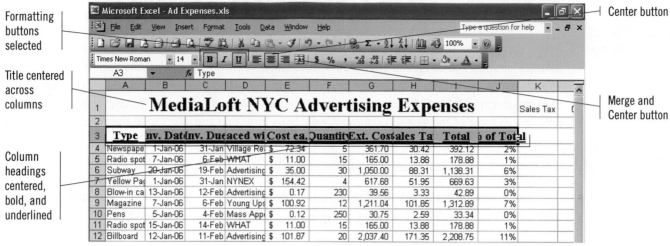

TABLE C-2: Attribute and alignment buttons on the Formatting toolbar

button	description	button	description
B	Bolds text	(align left)	Aligns text on the left side of the cell
I	Italicizes text	(center)	Centers text horizontally within the cell
U	Underlines text	(align right)	Aligns text on the right side of the cell
(borders)	Adds lines or borders	(merge)	Centers text across columns, and combines two or more selected, adjacent cells into one cell

Clues to Use

Using AutoFormat

Excel has 16 predefined worksheet formats to make formatting your worksheets easier and to give you the option of consistently styling your worksheets. AutoFormats are designed for worksheets with labels in the left column and top rows, and totals in the bottom row or right column. To use AutoFormat, select the data to be formatted—or place your mouse pointer anywhere within the range to be selected (Excel can automatically detect a range of cells)—click Format on the menu bar, click AutoFormat, select a format from the sample boxes in the AutoFormat dialog box, as shown in Figure C-8, then click OK.

FIGURE C-8: AutoFormat dialog box

Samples of
available
formats

Adjusting Column Widths

As you continue formatting a worksheet, you might need to adjust column widths to accommodate a larger font size or style. The default column width is 8.43 characters wide, a little less than one inch. With Excel, you can adjust the column width for one or more columns by using the mouse or the Column command on the Format menu. Table C-3 describes the commands available on the Format Column menu. Jim notices that some of the labels in column A have been truncated and don't fit in the cells. He asks you to adjust the widths of the columns so that the labels appear in their entirety.

STEPS

1. **Position the pointer on the line between the column A and column B headings**

   The **column heading** is the orange box at the top of each column containing a letter. The pointer changes to ↔, as shown in Figure C-9. You position the pointer on the right edge of the column that you are adjusting. The Yellow Pages entries are the widest in the column.

   QUICK TIP
   To reset columns to the default width, click the column headings to select the columns, click Format on the menu bar, point to Column, click Standard Width in the Column Width dialog box, then click OK.

2. **Click and drag the ↔ pointer to the right until the column displays the Yellow Pages entries fully**

   You can use the **AutoFit** feature and your mouse to resize a column so it automatically accommodates the widest entry in a cell.

3. **Position the pointer on the column line between columns B and C headings until it changes to ↔, then double-click**

   Column B automatically widens to fit the widest entry, in this case, the column label.

4. **Use AutoFit to resize columns C, D, and J**

   You can also use the Column Width command on the Format menu to adjust several columns to the same width.

5. **Select the range F5:I5**

   Columns can be adjusted by selecting any cell in the column.

6. **Click Format on the menu bar, point to Column, click Width to open the Column Width dialog box, then move the dialog box, if necessary, by dragging it by its title bar so you can see the selected columns**

   The column width measurement is based on the number of characters in the Normal font (in this case, Arial).

   TROUBLE
   If "#######" appears after you adjust a column of values, the column is too narrow to display the contents. Increase the column width until the values appear.

7. **Type 11 in the Column Width text box, then click OK**

   The column widths change to reflect the new setting. See Figure C-10.

8. **Click the Save button 🖫 on the Standard toolbar**

TABLE C-3: Format Column commands

command	description
Width	Sets the width to a specific number of characters
AutoFit Selection	Fits to the widest entry
Hide	Hide(s) column(s)
Unhide	Unhide(s) column(s)
Standard Width	Resets width to default widths

FIGURE C-9: Preparing to change the column width

Resize pointer
between
columns
A and B

Row 2 button

Column D
button

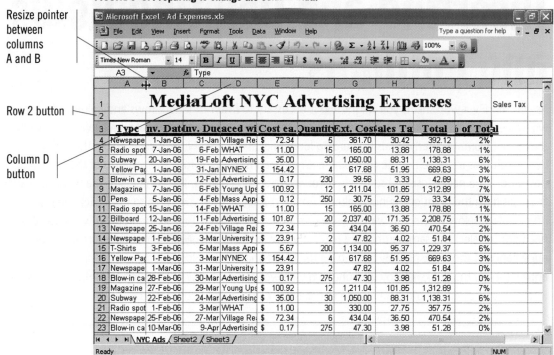

FIGURE C-10: Worksheet with column widths adjusted

Columns
widened
to display
text

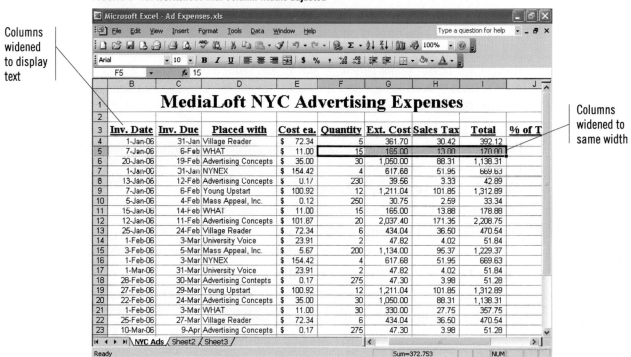

Columns
widened to
same width

Specifying row height

The Row Height command on the Format menu allows you to customize row height to improve readability. Row height is calculated in points, the same units of measure used for fonts. The row height must exceed the size of the font you are using. Normally, you don't need to adjust row heights manually. If you format something in a row to be a larger point size, Excel adjusts the row to fit the largest point size in the row. You can also adjust row height by placing the ⏚ pointer under the row heading and dragging to the desired height.

Inserting and Deleting Rows and Columns

As you modify a worksheet, you might find it necessary to insert or delete rows and columns to keep your worksheet current. For example, you might need to insert rows to accommodate new inventory products or remove a column of yearly totals that are no longer necessary. Excel inserts rows above the cell pointer and inserts columns to the left of the cell pointer. When you insert a new row, the contents of the worksheet shift down from the newly inserted row. When you insert a new column, the contents of the worksheet shift to the right from the point of the new column. To insert a single row, you can also right-click the row heading immediately below where you want the new row, then click Insert. To insert multiple rows, drag across row headings to select the same number of rows as you want to insert. ▓▓▓▓ You have already improved the appearance of the worksheet by formatting the labels and values. Now Jim asks you to improve the overall appearance of the worksheet by inserting a row between the last row of data and the totals. Also, you have located a row of inaccurate data and an unnecessary column that you need to delete.

STEPS

1. **Right-click cell A32, then click Insert on the shortcut menu**

   The Insert dialog box opens. See Figure C-11. You can choose to insert a column or a row, or you can shift the data in the cells in the active column right or in the active row down. An additional row between the last row of data and the totals will visually separate the totals.

QUICK TIP
Inserting or deleting rows or columns can cause problems in formulas that contain absolute cell references. After adding rows or columns to a worksheet, be sure to proof your formulas.

2. **Click the Entire row option button, then click OK**

   A blank row appears between the totals and the Billboard data, and the formula result in cell E33 has not changed. The Insert Options button 🖌 now appears beside cell A33. When you place ⬓ over 🖌, you can click the Insert Options list arrow and select from the following options: Format Same As Above, Format Same As Below, or Clear Formatting.

3. **Click the row 27 heading**

   Hats from Mass Appeal Inc. are no longer part of the advertising campaign. All of row 27 is selected, as shown in Figure C-12.

QUICK TIP
Use the Edit menu, or right-click the selected row and click Delete to remove a selected row. Pressing [Delete] on the keyboard removes the contents of a selected row; the row itself remains.

4. **Click Edit on the menu bar, then click Delete**

   Excel deletes row 27, and all rows below this shift up one row.

5. **Click the column J heading**

   The percentage information is calculated elsewhere and is no longer necessary in this worksheet.

6. **Click Edit on the menu bar, then click Delete**

   Excel deletes column J. The remaining columns to the right shift left one column.

7. **Click the Save button 🖫 on the Standard toolbar**

Clues to Use

Hiding and unhiding columns and rows

As you work with a worksheet, you may find that you need to make one or more columns or rows invisible. You can hide a selected column by clicking Format on the menu bar, pointing to Column, then clicking Hide. A hidden column is indicated by a black vertical line in its original position. You can display a hidden column by selecting the columns on either side of the black line, clicking Format on the menu bar, pointing to Column, and then clicking Unhide. (To hide/unhide one or more rows, substitute Row for the Column command.)

FIGURE C-11: Insert dialog box

Click here to insert a row →

FIGURE C-12: Worksheet with row 27 selected

Row 27 heading

Inserted row

Insert Options button might appear in a different location, or not at all

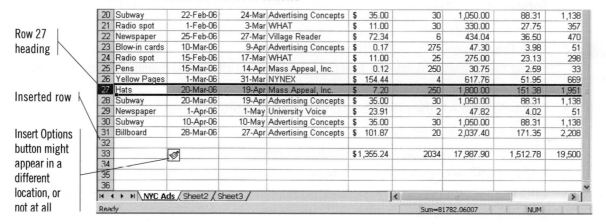

20	Subway	22-Feb-06	24-Mar	Advertising Concepts	$	35.00	30	1,050.00	88.31	1,138
21	Radio spot	1-Feb-06	3-Mar	WHAT	$	11.00	30	330.00	27.75	357
22	Newspaper	25-Feb-06	27-Mar	Village Reader	$	72.34	6	434.04	36.50	470
23	Blow-in cards	10-Mar-06	9-Apr	Advertising Concepts	$	0.17	275	47.30	3.98	51
24	Radio spot	15-Feb-06	17-Mar	WHAT	$	11.00	25	275.00	23.13	298
25	Pens	15-Mar-06	14-Apr	Mass Appeal, Inc.	$	0.12	250	30.75	2.59	33
26	Yellow Pages	1-Mar-06	31-Mar	NYNEX	$	154.44	4	617.76	51.95	669
27	Hats	20-Mar-06	19-Apr	Mass Appeal, Inc.	$	7.20	250	1,800.00	151.38	1,951
28	Subway	20-Mar-06	19-Apr	Advertising Concepts	$	35.00	30	1,050.00	88.31	1,138
29	Newspaper	1-Apr-06	1-May	University Voice	$	23.91	2	47.82	4.02	51
30	Subway	10-Apr-06	10-May	Advertising Concepts	$	35.00	30	1,050.00	88.31	1,138
31	Billboard	28-Mar-06	27-Apr	Advertising Concepts	$	101.87	20	2,037.40	171.35	2,208
32										
33					$1,355.24		2034	17,987.90	1,512.78	19,500
34										
35										
36										

|◄ ◄ ► ►| \ **NYC Ads** / Sheet2 / Sheet3 /

Ready   Sum=81782.06007   NUM

Clues to Use

Adding and editing comments

Much of your Excel work may be in collaboration with teammates with whom you share worksheets. You can share ideas with other worksheet users by adding comments within selected cells. To include a comment in a worksheet, click the cell where you want to place the comment, click Insert on the menu bar, then click Comment. A resizable text box containing the computer user's name opens in which you can type your comments. A small, red triangle appears in the upper-right corner of a cell containing a comment. If the comments are not already displayed, workbook users can point to the triangle to display the comment. To see all worksheet comments, as shown in Figure C-13, click View on the menu bar, then click Comments. To edit a comment, click the cell containing the comment, click Insert on the menu bar, then click Edit Comment. To delete a comment, right-click the cell containing the comment, then click Delete Comment on the shortcut menu.

FIGURE C-13: Comments in worksheet

20	Subway	22-Feb-06	24-Mar	Advertising Concepts	$	35.00
21	Radio spot	1-Feb-06	3-Mar	WHAT	$	11.00
22	Newspaper	25-Feb-06	27-Mar	Village Reader	$	72.34
23	Blow-in cards	10-Mar-06	9-Apr	Advertising Concepts	$	0.17
24	Radio spot	15-Feb-06	17-Mar		$	11.00
25	Pens	15-Mar-06	14-Apr		$	0.12
26	Yellow Pages	1-Mar-06	31-Mar		$	154.44
27	Subway	20-Mar-06	19-Apr		$	35.00
28	Newspaper	1-Apr-06	1-May	University Voice	$	23.91
29	Subway	10-Apr-06	10-May		$	35.00
30	Billboard	28-Mar-06	27-Apr		$	101.87
31						
32					$1,348.04
33						
34						
35						

Jim Fernandez: Should we continue with these ads, or expand to other publications?

Jim Fernandez: We need to evaluate whether we should continue these ads.

|◄ ◄ ► ►| \ **NYC Ads** / Sheet2 / Sheet3 /

Ready

Excel 2003

Applying Colors, Patterns, and Borders

You can use colors, patterns, and borders to enhance the overall appearance of a worksheet and to make it easier to read. You can add these enhancements by using the Patterns or Borders tabs in the Format Cells dialog box or by using the Borders and Color buttons on the Formatting toolbar. You can apply color or patterns to the background of a cell, to a range, or to cell contents. You can also apply borders to all the cells in a worksheet or only to selected cells to call attention to individual cells or groups of cells. See Table C-4 for a list of border buttons and their functions. Jim asks you to add a pattern, a border, and color to the title of the worksheet to give the worksheet a more professional appearance.

STEPS

1. **Press [Ctrl][Home] to select cell A1, then click the** Fill Color list arrow ⬛ **on the Formatting toolbar**

   The color palette appears.

2. **Click the** Turquoise color **(fourth row, fifth column)**

   Cell A1 has a turquoise background, as shown in Figure C-14. Cell A1 spans columns A through I because of the Merge and Center command used for the title.

   > **QUICK TIP**
   > Use color sparingly. Too much color can divert the reader's attention from the worksheet data.

3. **Right-click cell** A1, **then click** Format Cells **on the shortcut menu**

   The Format Cells dialog box opens.

4. **Click the** Patterns tab **if it is not already displayed**

   See Figure C-15. Adding a pattern to cells can add to the visual interest of your worksheet.

5. **Click the** Pattern list arrow, **click the** Thin Diagonal Crosshatch pattern **(third row, last column), then click** OK

   A border also enhances a cell's appearance. Unlike underlining, which is a text-formatting tool, borders extend to the width of the cell.

   > **QUICK TIP**
   > You can also draw cell borders using the mouse pointer. Click the Borders list arrow on the Formatting toolbar, click Draw Borders, then drag to create borders or boxes.

6. **Click the** Borders list arrow ⬛ **on the Formatting toolbar, then click the** Thick Bottom Border **(second row, second column)** ⬛ **on the Borders palette**

   It can be difficult to view a border in a selected cell.

7. **Click cell** A3

   The border is a nice enhancement. Font color can also help distinguish information in a worksheet.

   > **QUICK TIP**
   > The default color on the Fill Color and Font Color buttons changes to the last color you selected.

8. **Select the range** A3:I3, **click the** Font Color list arrow ⬛ **on the Formatting toolbar, then click the** Blue **color (second row, third column from the right) on the palette**

   The text changes color, as shown in Figure C-16.

9. **Click the** Save button ⬛ **on the Standard toolbar**

Clues to Use

Formatting columns or rows

You can save yourself time by formatting an entire column or row using any of the categories that appear in the Format Cells dialog box. You might, for example, want to format all the cells within a column to accept telephone numbers, social security numbers, zip codes, or custom number formats. Click the column or row heading—located at the top of a column or beginning of a row—to select the entire column or row. You can format a selected column or row by clicking Format on the menu bar, clicking Cells, then clicking the appropriate tab in the Format Cells dialog box.

FIGURE C-14: Background color added to cell

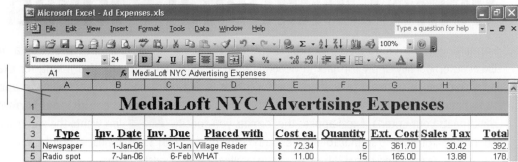

Cell A1 with
turquoise
background

FIGURE C-15: Patterns tab in the Format Cells dialog box

Sample of
selected color
and pattern

Pattern list arrow

FIGURE C-16: Worksheet with colors, patterns, and border

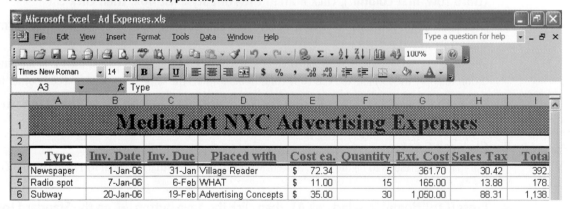

TABLE C-4: Border buttons

button	function	button	function	button	function
	No Border		Bottom Double Border		Top and Thick Bottom Border
	Bottom Border		Thick Bottom Border		All Borders
	Left Border		Top and Bottom Border		Outside Borders
	Right Border		Top and Double Bottom Border		Thick Box Border

FORMATTING A WORKSHEET EXCEL C-13

Using Conditional Formatting

Formatting makes worksheets look professional and helps distinguish different types of data. You can have Excel automatically apply formatting depending on specific values in cells. You might, for example, want advertising costs above a certain number to appear in red boldface and lower values to appear in blue. Automatically applying formatting attributes based on cell values is called **conditional formatting**. If the data meets your criteria, Excel applies the formats you specify. Jim wants the worksheet to include conditional formatting so that total advertising costs greater than $175 appear in boldface red type. He asks you to create the conditional format in the first cell in the Total cost column.

STEPS

1. **Click cell G4**

   Use the scroll bars if necessary, to make column G visible.

   TROUBLE

   If the Office Assistant appears, close it by clicking the No, don't provide help now button.

2. **Click Format on the menu bar, then click Conditional Formatting**

   The Conditional Formatting dialog box opens. Depending on the logical operator you've selected (such as "greater than" or "not equal to"), the Conditional Formatting dialog box displays different input boxes. You can define up to three different conditions, and then assign formatting attributes to each one. You define the condition first. The default setting for the first condition is "Cell Value Is" "between."

3. **Click the Operator list arrow to change the current condition, then click greater than or equal to**

   Because you changed the operator from "between," which required text boxes for two values, only one value text box now appears. The first condition is that the cell value must be greater than or equal to some value. See Table C-5 for a list of options. The value can be a constant, formula, cell reference, or date. That value is set in the third box.

4. **Click the Value text box, then type 175**

   Now that you have assigned the value, you need to specify what formatting you want for cells that meet this condition.

5. **Click Format, click the Color list arrow in the Format Cells dialog box, click the Red color (third row, first column), click Bold in the Font style list box, then click OK**

6. **Compare your settings to Figure C-17, then click OK to close the Conditional Formatting dialog box**

   The value in cell G4, 361.70, is formatted in bold red numbers because it is greater than 175, meeting the condition to apply the format. You can copy conditional formats the same way you would copy other formats.

7. **Verify that cell G4 is selected, click the Format Painter button 🖌 on the Standard toolbar, then drag ⊹🖌 to select the range G5:G30**

8. **Click cell G4**

   Compare your results to Figure C-18. All cells with values greater than or equal to 175 in column G appear in bold red text.

9. **Press [Ctrl][Home] to select cell A1, then click the Save button 🖫 on the Standard toolbar**

TABLE C–5: Conditional formatting options

option	mathematical equivalent	option	mathematical equivalent
Between	$X>Y<Z$	Greater than	$Z>Y$
Not between	$B>C<A$	Less than	$Y<Z$
Equal to	$A=B$	Greater than or equal to	$A>=B$
Not equal to	$A≠B$	Less than or equal to	$Z<=Y$

FIGURE C-17: Completed Conditional Formatting dialog box

Operator list arrow

Enter value in the Value text box

Click to define format of cells that meet the condition

Click to add additional condition(s)

Click to delete existing condition(s)

FIGURE C-18: Worksheet with conditional formatting

Format Painter button

Results of conditional formatting

Clues to Use

Deleting conditional formatting

Because it's likely that the conditions you define will change, you can delete any conditional format you define. Select the cell(s) containing conditional formatting, click Format on the menu bar, click Conditional Formatting, then click Delete in the Conditional Formatting dialog box. The Delete Conditional Format dialog box opens, as shown in Figure C-19. Select the check boxes for any of the conditions you want to delete, click OK, then click OK again. The previously assigned formatting is deleted—leaving the cell's contents intact.

FIGURE C-19: Delete Conditional Format dialog box

FORMATTING A WORKSHEET EXCEL C-15

UNIT
C
Excel 2003

Checking Spelling

A single misspelled word can cast doubt on the validity and professional value of your entire workbook. Excel includes a spelling checker to help you ensure that the words in your worksheet are spelled correctly. The spelling checker scans your worksheet, displays words it doesn't find in its built-in dictionary, and when possible, suggests replacements. To check other sheets in a multiple-sheet workbook, you need to display each sheet and run the spelling checker again. Because the built-in dictionary cannot possibly include all the words that anyone needs, you can add words to the dictionary, such as your company name, an acronym, or an unusual technical term. The spelling checker will no longer consider that word misspelled. Any words you've added to the dictionary using Word, Access, or PowerPoint are also available in Excel. Because he will distribute this workbook to the marketing managers, Jim asks you to check its spelling.

STEPS

TROUBLE
If a language other than English is being used, the Spelling dialog box lists the name of that language in its title bar.

1. **Click the** Spelling button **on the Standard toolbar**

   The Spelling: English (U.S.) dialog box opens, as shown in Figure C-21, with MediaLoft selected as the first misspelled word in the worksheet. For any word, you have the option to Ignore or to Ignore All cases that the spell checker flags, or to Add the word to the dictionary.

2. **Click** Ignore All **for MediaLoft**

   The spelling checker found the word "cards" misspelled and offers "crabs" as an alternative.

3. **Scroll through the Suggestions list, click** cards, **then click** Change

   The word "Concepts" is also misspelled, and the spelling checker suggests the correct spelling.

4. **Click** Change

   When no more incorrect words are found, Excel displays a message indicating that all the words on the worksheet have been checked.

5. **Click** OK

6. **Enter your name in cell** A34, **then press** [Ctrl][Home]

QUICK TIP
You can set **AutoCorrect** to correct spelling as you type. Click Tools on the menu bar, then click AutoCorrect Options.

7. **Click the** Save button **on the Standard toolbar, then preview the worksheet**

8. **In the Preview window, click** Setup **to open the Page Setup dialog box, under Scaling click** Fit to option button **to print the worksheet on one page, click** OK, **click** Print, **then click** OK

   Compare your printout to Figure C-22.

9. **Click** File **on the menu bar, then click** Exit **to close the workbook without saving changes and exit Excel**

Clues to Use

Using e-mail to send a workbook

Once you have checked for spelling errors, you can use e-mail to send an entire workbook from within Excel. To send a workbook as an e-mail message attachment, open the workbook, click File on the menu bar, point to Send To, then click Mail Recipient (as Attachment). You supply the To and optional Cc information, as shown in Figure C-20, then click Send.

FIGURE C-20: E-mailing an Excel workbook

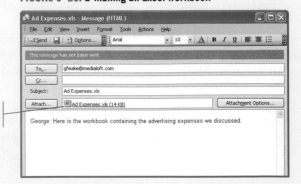

Workbook is automatically attached to message

FIGURE C-21: Spelling English dialog box

Misspelled word

Type replacement word here or click a suggestion

Click to ignore all occurrences of misspelled word

Click to add word to dictionary

FIGURE C-22: Completed worksheet

MediaLoft NYC Advertising Expenses

Sales Tax   0.0841

Type	Inv. Date	Inv. Due	Placed with	Cost ea.	Quantity	Ext. Cost	Sales Tax	Total
Newspaper	1-Jan-06	31-Jan	Village Reader	$ 72.34	5	361.70	30.42	392.12
Radio spot	7-Jan-06	6-Feb	WHAT	$ 11.00	15	165.00	13.88	178.88
Subway	20-Jan-06	19-Feb	Advertising Concepts	$ 35.00	30	1,050.00	88.31	1,138.31
Yellow Pages	1-Jan-06	31-Jan	NYNEX	$ 154.42	4	617.68	51.95	669.63
Blow-in cards	13-Jan-06	12-Feb	Advertising Concepts	$ 0.17	230	39.56	3.33	42.89
Magazine	7-Jan-06	6-Feb	Young Upstart	$ 100.92	12	1,211.04	101.85	1,312.89
Pens	5-Jan-06	4-Feb	Mass Appeal, Inc.	$ 0.12	250	30.75	2.59	33.34
Radio spot	15-Jan-06	14-Feb	WHAT	$ 11.00	15	165.00	13.88	178.88
Billboard	12-Jan-06	11-Feb	Advertising Concepts	$ 101.87	20	2,037.40	171.35	2,208.75
Newspaper	25-Jan-06	24-Feb	Village Reader	$ 72.34	6	434.04	36.50	470.54
Newspaper	1-Feb-06	3-Mar	University Voice	$ 23.91	2	47.82	4.02	51.84
T-Shirts	3-Feb-06	5-Mar	Mass Appeal, Inc.	$ 5.67	200	1,134.00	95.37	1,229.37
Yellow Pages	1-Feb-06	3-Mar	NYNEX	$ 154.42	4	617.68	51.95	669.63
Newspaper	1-Mar-06	31-Mar	University Voice	$ 23.91	2	47.82	4.02	51.84
Blow-in cards	28-Feb-06	30-Mar	Advertising Concepts	$ 0.17	275	47.30	3.98	51.28
Magazine	27-Feb-06	29-Mar	Young Upstart	$ 100.92	12	1,211.04	101.85	1,312.89
Subway	22-Feb-06	24-Mar	Advertising Concepts	$ 35.00	30	1,050.00	88.31	1,138.31
Radio spot	1-Feb-06	3-Mar	WHAT	$ 11.00	30	330.00	27.75	357.75
Newspaper	25-Feb-06	27-Mar	Village Reader	$ 72.34	6	434.04	36.50	470.54
Blow-in cards	10-Mar-06	9-Apr	Advertising Concepts	$ 0.17	275	47.30	3.98	51.28
Radio spot	15-Feb-06	17-Mar	WHAT	$ 11.00	25	275.00	23.13	298.13
Pens	15-Mar-06	14-Apr	Mass Appeal, Inc.	$ 0.12	250	30.75	2.59	33.34
Yellow Pages	1-Mar-06	31-Mar	NYNEX	$ 154.44	4	617.76	51.95	669.71
Subway	20-Mar-06	19-Apr	Advertising Concepts	$ 35.00	30	1,050.00	88.31	1,138.31
Newspaper	1-Apr-06	1-May	University Voice	$ 23.91	2	47.82	4.02	51.84
Subway	10-Apr-06	10-May	Advertising Concepts	$ 35.00	30	1,050.00	88.31	1,138.31
Billboard	28-Mar-06	27-Apr	Advertising Concepts	$ 101.87	20	2,037.40	171.35	2,208.75
				$ 1,348.04	1784	16,187.90	1,361.40	17,549.30

Your Name

Excel 2003

Practice

▼ CONCEPTS REVIEW

Label each element of the Excel worksheet window shown in Figure C-23.

FIGURE C-23

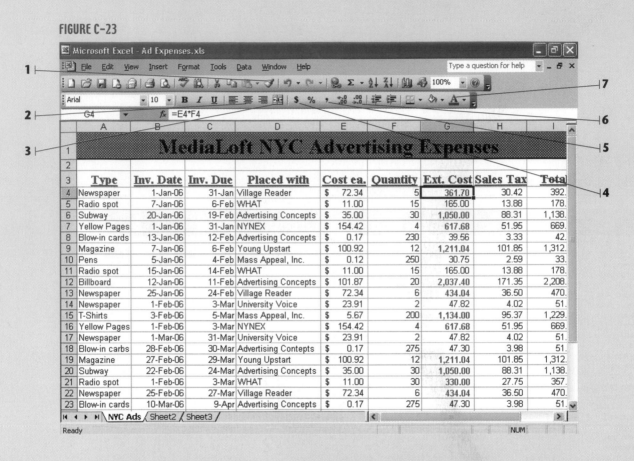

Match each command or button with the statement that best describes it.

8. $
9. ▣
10. ✓

11. Cells command on the Format menu
12. Conditional Formatting
13. Delete command on the Edit menu

a. Changes appearance of a cell depending on result
b. Erases the contents of a cell
c. Used to check the spelling in a worksheet
d. Used to change the appearance of selected cells
e. Pastes the contents of the Clipboard into the current cell
f. Changes the format to Currency

Select the best answer from the list of choices.

14. What is the name of the feature used to resize a column to its widest entry?
- **a.** AutoResize
- **b.** AutoFormat
- **c.** AutoFit
- **d.** AutoAdjust

15. Which button center-aligns the contents of a single cell?
- **a.** ⊞
- **b.** ▤
- **c.** ▤
- **d.** ▤

16. Which button increases the number of decimal places in selected cells?
- **a.** ⊞
- **b.** ⊞
- **c.** ◿
- **d.** ,

17. Which of the following is an example of the comma format?
- **a.** 5555.55
- **b.** 55.55%
- **c.** 5,555.55
- **d.** $5,555.55

18. How many conditional formats can be created in any cell?
- **a.** 1
- **b.** 2
- **c.** 3
- **d.** 4

19. Which feature applies formatting attributes according to cell contents?
- **a.** AutoFormat
- **b.** Comments
- **c.** Conditional Formatting
- **d.** Merge and Center

20. Each of the following operators can be used in conditional formatting, *except*:
- **a.** Equal to.
- **b.** Greater than.
- **c.** Similar to.
- **d.** Not between.

▼ SKILLS REVIEW

1. Format values.

a. Start Excel and open a new workbook.

b. Enter the information from Table C-6 in your worksheet. Begin in cell A1, and do not leave any blank rows or columns.

c. Save this workbook as **MediaLoft GB Sales** in the drive and folder where your Data Files are stored.

d. Select the range of values in the Average Price column.

e. Format the range using the Currency Style button.

f. Apply the Comma format to the Average Price and Quantity data, and reduce the number of decimals in the Quantity column to 0.

g. Insert formulas in the Totals column (multiply the Average Price by the Quantity).

h. Apply the Currency format to the Totals data.

i. Save your work.

TABLE C-6

MediaLoft Great Britain Quarterly Sales Projections			
Department	Average Price	Quantity	Totals
Sports	30	2250	
Computers	42	3185	
History	37	1325	
Personal Growth	29	2070	

2. Use fonts and font sizes.

a. Select the range of cells containing the column labels.

b. Change the font of the column labels to Times New Roman.

c. Increase the font size of the column labels and the label in cell A1 to 14 point.

d. Resize the columns as necessary.

e. Save your changes.

3. Change attributes and alignment.

a. Select the worksheet title **MediaLoft Great Britain**, then use the Bold button to apply the bold attribute.

b. Use the Merge and Center button to center the title and the Quarterly Sales Projections labels over columns A through D.

c. Select the label **Quarterly Sales Projections**, then apply underlining to the label.

d. Add the bold attribute to the labels in the Department column.

e. Use the Format Painter to paste the format from the data in the Department column to the Department and Totals labels.

f. Add the italics attribute to the Average Price and Quantity labels.

g. Select the range of cells containing the column titles, then center them.

h. Return the underlined, merged and centered Quarterly Sales Projections label to its original alignment.

i. Move the Quarterly Sales Projections label to cell D2 and change the alignment to Align Right.

j. Save your changes.

4. Adjust column widths.

   a. Use the Format menu to change the width of the Average Price column to **25**.

   b. Use the AutoFit feature to resize the Average Price column.

   c. Use the Format menu to resize the Department column to **18** and the Quantity column to **15**.

   d. Change the text in cell C3 to **Sold**, then use AutoFit to resize the column.

   e. Save your changes.

5. Insert and delete rows and columns.

   a. Insert a new row between rows 4 and 5.

   b. Add MediaLoft Great Britain's newest department—**Children's Corner**—in the newly inserted row. Enter **35** for the average price and **1225** for the number sold.

   c. Add the following comment to cell A5: **New department**. Display the comment, if necessary.

   d. Add a formula in cell D5 that multiplies the Average Price column by the Sold column.

   e. Add a new column between the Department and Average Price columns with the title **Location**.

   f. Delete the History row.

   g. Edit the comment in cell A5 so it reads "New department. Needs promotion."

   h. Save your changes.

6. Apply colors, patterns, and borders.

   a. Add an outside border around the Average Price and Sold data.

   b. Apply a light green background color to the labels in the Department column.

   c. Apply a gold background to the column labels in cells **A3:E3**.

   d. Change the color of the font in the column labels in cells A3:E3 to blue.

   e. Add a 12.5% Gray pattern fill to the title in cell A1. (*Hint*: Use the Patterns tab in the Format Cells dialog box to locate the 12.5% Gray pattern.)

   f. Enter your name in cell A20, then save your work.

   g. Preview and print the worksheet, then close the workbook.

7. Use conditional formatting.

   a. Open the file EX C-2.xls from the drive and folder where your Data Files are stored, then save it as **Monthly Operating Expenses**.

   b. Create conditional formatting that changes a monthly data entry to blue if the value is **greater than 2500**, and changes the monthly data entry to red if the value is **less than 700**.

   c. Create a third conditional format that changes the monthly data to green if a value is **between 1000 and 2000**.

   d. Use the Bold button and Center button to format the column headings and row titles.

   e. Make Column A wide enough to accommodate the contents of cells **A4:A9**.

   f. Create formulas in cells F4:F9 and cells B11:F11. Use the Comma Style with no decimals in these cells.

   g. AutoFit the remaining columns.

   h. Use Merge and Center in row 1 to center the title over columns A–F.

   i. Format the title in cell A1 using 14-point text. Fill the cell with a color and pattern of your choice.

   j. Delete the third conditional format.

   k. Enter your name in cell A20, then apply a green background to it and make the text color yellow.

   l. Use the Edit menu to clear the cell formats from the cell with your name, then save your changes.

8. Check spelling.

   a. Check the spelling in the worksheet using the spelling checker, correcting any spelling errors.

   b. Save your changes, then preview and print the workbook.

   c. Close the workbook, then exit Excel.

Excel 2003

▼ INDEPENDENT CHALLENGE 1

Beautiful You, a small beauty salon, has been using Excel for several months. Now that the salon's accounting records are in Excel, the manager would like you to work on the inventory. Although more items will be added later, the worksheet has enough items for you to begin your modifications.

a. Start Excel, open the file EX C-3.xls from the drive and folder where your Data Files are stored, then save it as **BY Inventory**.

b. Create a formula that calculates the value of the inventory on hand for each item.

c. Use an absolute reference to calculate the sale price of each item, using the markup percentage shown.

d. Add the bold attribute to the column headings.

e. Make sure all columns are wide enough to display the data and headings.

f. Change the On Hand Value and Sale Price columns so they display the Currency style with two decimal places.

g. Change the Price Paid column so it displays the Comma style with two decimal places.

h. Add a row under #2 Curlers for **Nail Files**, price paid **$0.25**, sold **individually (each)**, with **59** on hand.

i. Verify that all the formulas in the worksheet are correct. Adjust any items as needed, and check the spelling.

j. Use conditional formatting to call attention to items with a quantity of 25 or fewer on hand. Use boldfaced red text.

k. Add an outside border around the data in the Item column.

l. Delete the row with #3 Curlers.

m. Enter your name in an empty cell, then save the file.

n. Preview and print the worksheet, compare your work to the sample shown in Figure C-24, close the workbook, then exit Excel.

FIGURE C-24

	A	B	C	D	E	F	G	H	I	J
1	Beautiful You Salon						markup ->	1.35		
2										
3	**Item**	**Price Paid**	**Sold by**	**On Hand**	**On Hand Value**	**Sale Price**				
4	#2 Curlers	13.80	box	53	$ 731.40	$ 18.63				
5	Nail Files	0.25	each	59	$ 14.75	$ 0.34				
6	Hair dryers	4.25	each	75	$ 318.75	$ 5.74				
7	Nail polish	3.92	each	62	$ 243.04	$ 5.29				
8	Conditioner	2.99	each	35	$ 104.65	$ 4.04				
9	Scrumptious shampoo	8.30	each	25	$ 207.50	$ 11.21				
10	Clips	2.25	box	33	$ 74.25	$ 3.04				
11	Pins	4.75	box	36	$ 171.00	$ 6.41				
12	#1 Curlers	2.10	box	37	$ 77.70	$ 2.84				
13	Jumbo conditioner	10.65	each	22	$ 234.30	$ 14.38				
14	#472 color	16.32	each	13	$ 212.16	$ 22.03				
15										
16										
17										
18										
19										
20	Your Name									
21										
22										
23										
24										
25										

Sheet1 / Sheet2 / Sheet3 /

Ready   NUM

▼ INDEPENDENT CHALLENGE 2

You volunteer several hours each week with the Community Action Center. You would like to examine the membership list, and decide to use formatting to make the existing data look more professional and easier to read.

    a. Start Excel, open the file EX C-4.xls from the drive and folder where your Data Files are stored, then save it as **Community Action**.

    b. Remove any blank columns.

    c. Format the Annual Revenue figures using the Currency format.

    d. Make all columns wide enough to fit their data and headings.

    e. Use formatting enhancements, such as fonts, font sizes, and text attributes to make the worksheet more attractive.

    f. Center-align the column labels.

    g. Use conditional formatting so that entries for Number of Employees that are greater than 50 appear in a contrasting color.

    h. Adjust any items as necessary, then check the spelling.

    i. Enter your name in an empty cell, then save your work.

    j. Before printing, preview the file so you know what the worksheet looks like, then print a copy. Compare your work to the sample shown in Figure C-25.

    k. Close the workbook, then exit Excel.

FIGURE C-25

	A	B	C	D	E	F	G
1	Community Action Center Members						
2							
3		Annual	Number of		Type of		
4	Member	Revenue	Employees	Status	Business		
5	Lisa's Photo Studio	$ 56,000.00	5	member	Restaurant		
6	Chip Technology	$ 492,600.00	175	member	Manufacturing, Microchips		
7	Computer Attic	$ 128,000.00	4	member	Computer Consultant		
8	Deluxe Auto Shop	$ 98,420.00	7	member	Automotive		
9	Front Office	$ 162,320.00	25	member	Employment Agency		
10	General Hospital	$ 1,154,000.00	480	member	Health		
11	Grande Table	$ 101,500.00	25	member	Restaurant		
12	Holiday Inn	$ 175,000.00	75	member	Hotel/Motel		
13	Midas Muffler	$ 106,000.00	22	member	Automotive		
14	Mill Shoppe	$ 346,000.00	165	member	Manufacturing, Furniture		
15	Reservation Inn	$ 272,000.00	42	member	Hotel/Motel		
16	State University	$ 975,630.00	422	member	Education		
17	Candy's Candy Shop	$ 100,500.00	3	non-member	Restaurant		
18	Dental Associates	$ 175,000.00	15	non-member	Health		
19	Dr. Rachel	$ 173,000.00	5	non-member	Health		
20	Dunkin' Donuts	$ 66,420.00	7	non-member	Restaurant		
21	Earl's Restaurant	$ 290,000.00	45	non-member	Restaurant		
22	First Federal Bank	$ 1,216,500.00	36	non-member	Bank		
23	Friendly Chevy	$ 289,000.00	17	non-member	Automotive		
24	Ken's Florist Shop	$ 89,900.00	10	non-member	Florist		
25	Maineka Muffler	$ 107,900.00	24	non-member	Automotive		

Sheet1 / Sheet2 / Sheet3 /

Ready   NUM

▼ INDEPENDENT CHALLENGE 3

Classic Instruments is a Miami-based company that manufactures high-quality pens and markers. As the finance manager, one of your responsibilities is to analyze the monthly reports from your five district sales offices. Your boss, Joanne Bennington, has just asked you to prepare a quarterly sales report for an upcoming meeting. Because several top executives will be attending this meeting, Joanne reminds you that the report must look professional. In particular, she asks you to emphasize the company's surge in profits during the last month and to highlight the fact that the Northeastern district continues to outpace the other districts.

a. Plan a worksheet that shows the company's sales during the first quarter. Assume that all pens are the same price. Make sure you include:

- The number of pens sold (units sold) and the associated revenues (total sales) for each of the five district sales offices. The five sales districts are: Northeastern, Midwestern, Southeastern, Southern, and Western.
- Calculations that show month-by-month totals and a three-month cumulative total
- Calculations that show each district's share of sales (percent of Total Sales)
- Formatting enhancements to emphasize the recent month's sales surge and the Northeastern district's sales leadership

b. Ask yourself the following questions about the organization and formatting of the worksheet: How can you calculate the totals? What formulas can you copy to save time and keystrokes? Do any of these formulas need to use an absolute reference? How do you show dollar amounts? What information should be shown in bold? Do you need to use more than one font? Should you use more than one point size?

c. Start Excel, then build the worksheet with your own price and sales data. Enter the titles and labels first, then enter the numbers and formulas. You can use the information in Table C-7 to get started.

TABLE C-7:

Classic Instruments 1st Quarter Sales Report		January		February		March		Total	
Office	Price	Units Sold	Sales	Units Sold	Sales	Units Sold	Sales	Units Sold	Sales
Northeastern									
Midwestern									
Southeastern									
Southern									
Western									

d. Save the workbook as **Classic Instruments** in the drive and folder where your Data Files are stored.

e. Adjust the column widths as necessary.

f. Change the height of row 1 to 30 points.

g. Format labels and values, and change the attributes and alignment if necessary.

h. Resize columns and adjust the formatting as necessary.

i. Add a column that calculates a 24% increase in sales dollars. Use an absolute cell reference in this calculation.

j. Create a new column named Increase in Sales that adds the projected increase to the Total Sales. (*Hint*: Make sure the current formatting is applied to the new information.)

Advanced Challenge Exercise

- Use AutoFormat to add color and formatting to the data.
- Insert a clip art image in an appropriate location, adjusting its size and position as necessary.

k. Enter your name in an empty cell.

l. Check the spelling, then save your work.

m. Preview, then print the file in landscape orientation.

n. Close the file, then exit Excel.

▼ INDEPENDENT CHALLENGE 4

After saving for many years, you now have enough funds to take that international trip you have always dreamed about. Your well-traveled friends have told you that you should always have the local equivalent of $100 U.S. dollars in cash with you when you enter a country. You decide to use the Web to determine how much money you will need in each country.

a. Start Excel, open a new workbook, then save it as **Currency Conversions** in the drive and folder where your Data Files are stored.

b. Enter column and row labels using the information in Table C-8 to get started.

c. Use your favorite search engine to find your own information sources on currency conversions.

d. Find out how much cash is equivalent to **$1** in U.S. dollars for the following countries: **Australia**, **Canada**, **France**, **Germany**, **Sweden**, and the **United Kingdom**. Also enter the name of the currency used in each country.

e. Create an equation that calculates the equivalent of **$100** in U.S. dollars for each country in the list, using an absolute value in the formula.

f. Format the entries in columns B and C using the correct currency unit for each country, with two decimal places. (*Hint*: Use the Numbers tab in the Format cells dialog box; choose the appropriate currency format from the Symbol list, using two decimal places.)

TABLE C-8

Currency Equivalents $100 in US dollars			
Country	$1 Equivalent	$100 US	Name of Units
Australia			
Canada			
France			
Germany			
Sweden			
United Kingdom			

g. Create a conditional format that changes the font attributes of the calculated amount in the "$100 US" column to bold and red if the amount is equals or exceeds **500 units** of the local currency.

h. Merge and center the title over the column headings.

i. Add any formatting attributes to the column headings, and resize the columns as necessary.

j. Add a background color to the title.

Advanced Challenge Exercise

- Apply the AutoFormat of your choice to the conversion table.
- Delete the conditional format in the $100 US column.
- If you have access to an e-mail account, e-mail this workbook to your instructor as an attachment.

k. Enter your name in an empty worksheet cell.

l. Spell check, save, preview, then print the worksheet.

m. Close the workbook and exit Excel.

▼ VISUAL WORKSHOP

Create the worksheet shown in Figure C-26, using skills you learned in this unit. Open the file EX C-5.xls from the drive and folder where your Data Files are stored, then save it as **Projected March Advertising Invoices**. Create a conditional format in the Cost ea. column so that entries greater than 60 appear in red. (*Hint*: The only additional font used in this exercise is Times New Roman. It is 22 point in row 1, and 16 point in row 3.) Enter your name in cell A20, spell check the worksheet, then save and print your work.

FIGURE C-26

Working with Charts

OBJECTIVES

Plan and design a chart
Create a chart
Move and resize a chart
Edit a chart
Format a chart
Enhance a chart
Annotate and draw on a chart
Preview and print a chart

If you have a SAM user profile, you may have access to hands-on instruction, practice, and assessment of the skills covered in this unit. Log in to your SAM account and go to your assignments page to see what your instructor has assigned.

Worksheets provide an effective way to organize information, but they are not always the best format for presenting data to others. Information in a selected range or worksheet can easily be displayed as a chart. **Charts**, often called graphs, allow you to communicate the relationships in your worksheet data in readily understandable pictures. In this unit, you will learn how to create a chart, how to edit a chart and change the chart type, how to add text annotations and arrows to a chart, and how to preview and print a chart. For the annual meeting, Jim Fernandez needs you to create a chart showing the six-month sales history for the MediaLoft stores in the Eastern Division. He wants to illustrate the growth trend in this division.

Planning and Designing a Chart

Before creating a chart, you need to plan the information you want your chart to show and how you want it to look. ▄▄▄▄▄ In early June, the Marketing Department launched a regional advertising campaign for the Eastern Division. The results of the campaign were increased sales during the fall months. Jim wants you to create a chart for the annual meeting that illustrates the growth trend for sales in MediaLoft's Eastern Division stores and to highlight this sales increase.

DETAILS

Jim wants you to use the worksheet shown in Figure D-1 and the following guidelines to plan the chart:

- **Determine the purpose of the chart and identify the data relationships you want to communicate graphically**

    You want to create a chart that shows sales throughout MediaLoft's Eastern Division from July through December. In particular, you want to highlight the increase in sales that occurred as a result of the advertising campaign.

- **Determine the results you want to see, and decide which chart type is most appropriate to use**

    Different charts display data in distinctive ways. Some chart types are more appropriate for particular types of data and analyses. How you want your data displayed—and how you want that data interpreted—can help you determine the best chart type to use. Table D-1 describes several different types of charts, the corresponding button on the Chart Type palette located on the Chart toolbar, and indicates when each one is best used. Because you want to compare data (sales in multiple locations) over a time period (the months July through December), you decide to use a column chart.

- **Identify the worksheet data you want the chart to illustrate**

    You are using data from the worksheet titled MediaLoft Eastern Division Stores shown in Figure D-1. This worksheet contains the sales data for the four stores in the Eastern Division from July through December.

- **Sketch the chart, then use your sketch to decide where the chart elements should be placed**

    You sketch your chart as shown in Figure D-2. You put the months on the horizontal axis (the **x-axis**) and the monthly sales figures on the vertical axis (the **y-axis**). The x-axis is often called the **category axis** because it often contains the names of data groups, such as months or years. The y-axis is called the **value axis** because it often contains numerical values that help you interpret the size of chart elements. (In a 3-D chart, the y-axis is referred to as the z-axis.) The area inside the horizontal and vertical axes is called the **plot area**. The **tick marks** on the y-axis create a scale of measure for each value. Each value in a cell you select for your chart is a **data point**. In any chart, a **data marker** visually represents each data point, which in this case is a column. A collection of related data points is a **data series**. In this chart, there are four data series (Boston, Chicago, Kansas City, and New York), so you include a **legend** to make it easy to identify them.

FIGURE D-1: Worksheet containing sales data

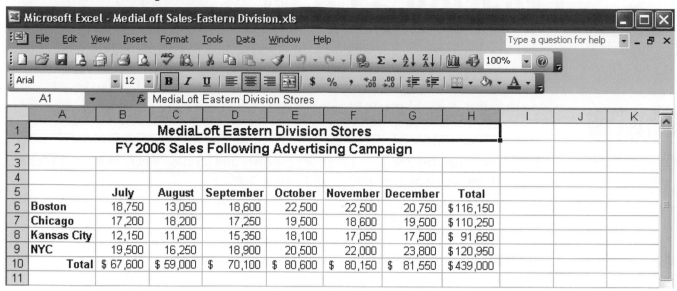

FIGURE D-2: Column chart sketch

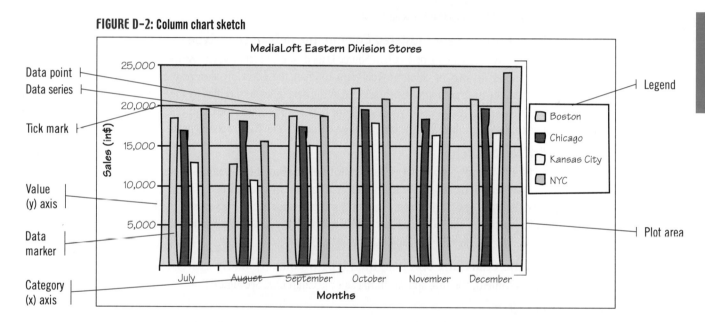

TABLE D-1: Commonly used chart types

type	button	description
Area		Shows how individual volume changes over time in relation to total volume
Bar		Compares distinct object levels over time using a horizontal format; sometimes referred to as a horizontal bar chart in other spreadsheet programs
Column		Compares distinct object levels over time using a vertical format; the Excel default; sometimes referred to as a bar chart in other spreadsheet programs
Line		Compares trends over even time intervals; appears similar to an area chart, but does not emphasize total
Pie		Compares sizes of pieces as part of a whole; used for a single series of numbers
XY (scatter)		Compares trends over uneven time or measurement intervals; used in scientific and engineering disciplines for trend spotting and extrapolation
Combination	none	Combines a column and line chart to compare data requiring different scales of measure

Creating a Chart

To create a chart in Excel, you first select the range containing the data you want to chart. Once you've selected a range, you can use the Excel **Chart Wizard** to lead you through the process of creating the chart. ▰▰▰▰ Using the worksheet containing the sales data for the Eastern Division, Jim asks you to create a chart that shows the growth trend that occurred.

STEPS

QUICK TIP
When charting any data, make sure all series are for the same time period.

1. **Start Excel, open the File** EX D-1.xls **from the drive and location where your Data Files are stored, then save it as** MediaLoft Sales-Eastern Division

   You want the chart to include the monthly sales figures for each of the Eastern Division stores, as well as month and store labels. You don't include the Total column and row because the monthly figures make up the totals, and these figures would skew the chart.

QUICK TIP
You can create a chart from noncontiguous cells by pressing and holding [Ctrl] while selecting each range.

2. **Select the range** A5:G9, **then click the** Chart Wizard button 📊 **on the Standard toolbar**

   The selected range contains the data you want to chart. The Chart Wizard opens. The Chart Wizard - Step 1 of 4 - Chart Type dialog box lets you choose the type of chart you want to create. The default chart type is a Clustered Column, as shown in Figure D-3. You can see a preview of the chart using your selected data by pressing and holding the Press and Hold to View Sample button.

3. **Click** Next **to accept Clustered Column, the default chart type**

   The Chart Wizard - Step 2 of 4 - Chart Source Data dialog box lets you choose the data to chart and whether the series appear in rows or columns. You want to chart the effect of sales for each store over the time period. Currently, the rows are appropriately selected as the data series, as specified by the Series in option button (located under the Data range). Because you selected the data before clicking the Chart Wizard button, Excel converted the range to absolute values and the correct range, =Sheet1!$A$5:$G$9, appears in the Data range text box.

4. **Click** Next

   The Chart Wizard - Step 3 of 4 - Chart Options dialog box shows a sample chart using the data you selected. The store locations (the rows in the selected range) are plotted against the months (the columns in the selected range), and Excel added the months as labels for each data series. A legend shows each location and its corresponding color on the chart. The Titles tab lets you add titles to the chart and its axes. Other tabs let you modify the axes, legend, and other chart elements.

5. **Click the** Chart title text box, **then type** MediaLoft Sales - Eastern Division

   After a moment, the title appears in the Sample Chart box. See Figure D-4.

6. **Click** Next

   In the Chart Wizard - Step 4 of 4 - Chart Location dialog box, you determine the placement of the chart in the workbook. You can display a chart as an object on the current sheet (called an **embedded chart**), on any other existing sheet, or on a newly created chart sheet. A **chart sheet** in a workbook contains only a chart, which is linked to the workbook data. The default selection—displaying the chart as an object in the sheet containing the data—will help Jim emphasize his point at the annual meeting.

QUICK TIP
If the Chart toolbar does not display, click View on the menu bar, point to Toolbars, and then click Chart.

7. **Click** Finish

   The column chart appears and the Chart toolbar opens, either docked or floating, as shown in Figure D-5. Your chart and the chart toolbar might be in different locations, and the chart may look slightly different. You adjust the chart's location and size in the next lesson. The **sizing handles**, the small squares at the corners and sides of the chart's border, indicate that the chart is selected. Any time a chart is selected, as it is now, a blue border surrounds the worksheet data range, a green border surrounds the row labels, and a purple border surrounds the column labels.

8. **Click the** Save button 💾 **on the Standard toolbar**

FIGURE D-3: First Chart Wizard dialog box

Selected chart

Chart types

Clustered column chart is the default

Chart sub-types for selected chart

Description of selected chart sub-type

FIGURE D-4: Third Chart Wizard dialog box

Type the chart title here

Sample chart

Title added

Legend

FIGURE D-5: Worksheet with column chart

Column labels

Row labels

Data range

Selected chart object

Chart toolbar

Title

Legend

Sizing handles

Month labels on the x-axis

Moving and Resizing a Chart

Charts are graphics, or drawn objects, and are not located in a specific cell or at a specific range address. An **object** is an independent element on a worksheet. You can select an object by clicking within its borders to surround it with sizing handles. You can move a selected chart object anywhere on a worksheet without affecting formulas or data in the worksheet. However, any data changed in the worksheet is automatically updated in the chart. You can resize a chart to improve its appearance by dragging its sizing handles. You can even put a chart on another sheet, and it will still reflect the original data. Chart objects contain other objects, such as a title and legend, which you can move and resize. To move an object, select it, then drag it or cut and copy it to a new location. When you select a chart object, the name of the selected object appears in the Chart Objects list box on the Chart toolbar and in the Name box. ▓▓▓▓ Jim wants you to increase the size of the chart, position it below the worksheet data, and reposition the legend.

STEPS

QUICK TIP

If you want to delete a chart, select it, then press [Delete].

1. **Make sure the chart is still selected, then position the pointer over the chart**

   The pointer shape ⟍ indicates that you can move the chart or use a sizing handle to resize it. For a table of commonly used chart pointers, refer to Table D-2. On occasion, the Chart toolbar obscures your view. You can dock the toolbar to make it easier to see your work.

2. **If the chart toolbar is floating, click the Chart toolbar's title bar, drag it to the right edge of the status bar until it docks, then release the mouse button**

   The toolbar is docked on the bottom of the screen.

3. **Place ⟍ on a blank area near the edge of the chart, press and hold the left mouse button, using ✛, drag the chart until its upper-left edge is at the top of row 13 and the left edge of the chart is at the left border of column A, then release the mouse button**

   As you drag the chart, you can see a dotted outline representing the chart's perimeter. The chart appears in the new location.

QUICK TIP

Resizing a chart doesn't affect the data in the chart, only the way the chart looks on the sheet.

4. **Position the pointer on the right-middle sizing handle until it changes to ↔, then drag the right edge of the chart to the right edge of column H**

   The chart is widened. See Figure D-6.

5. **Position the pointer over the upper-middle sizing handle until it changes to ↕, then drag it to the top edge of row 12**

6. **Scroll down the screen, position the pointer over the lower-middle sizing handle until it changes to ↕, then drag to position the bottom border of the chart at the bottom border of row 25**

   You can move the legend to improve the chart's appearance. You want to align the top of the legend with the top of the plot area.

QUICK TIP

Placing the mouse pointer over a chart object displays a ScreenTip identifying it, whether the chart is selected or not. If a chart—or any object in it—is selected, the ScreenTips still appear and the name of the selected chart object appears in the Chart Objects list box on the Chart toolbar and in the Name box.

7. **Click the legend to select it, then drag the legend upward using ⟍ so the top of the legend aligns with the top of the plot area**

   Sizing handles appear around the legend when you click it; "Legend" appears in the Chart Objects list box on the Chart toolbar as well as in the Name box, and a dotted outline of the legend border appears as you drag. Changing any label modifies the legend text.

8. **Click cell A9, type NYC, then click the Enter button ✓ on the formula bar**

   See Figure D-7. The legend changes to the text you entered. Because the chart is no longer selected, the chart toolbar no longer appears at the bottom of the screen.

9. **Click the Save button 🖫 on the Standard toolbar**

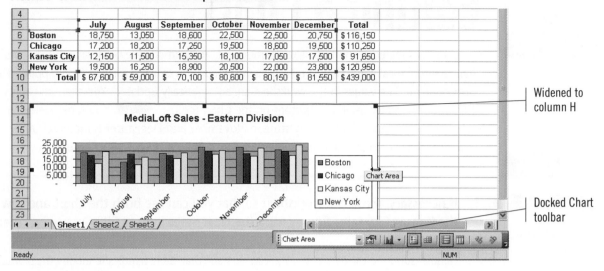

FIGURE D-6: Worksheet with resized and repositioned chart

Widened to column H

Docked Chart toolbar

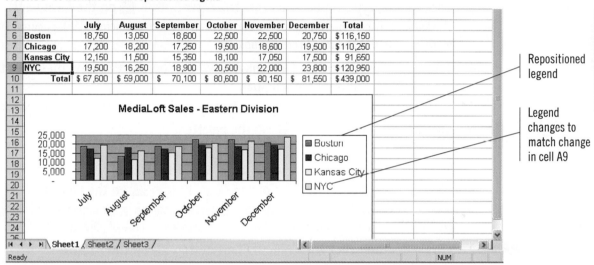

FIGURE D-7: Worksheet with repositioned legend

Repositioned legend

Legend changes to match change in cell A9

TABLE D-2: Commonly used pointers

name	pointer	use	name	pointer	use
Diagonal resizing	↗ or ↘	Change chart shape	I-beam	I	Edit chart text from corners
Draw	+	Create shapes	Move chart	✛	Change chart location
Horizontal resizing	↔	Change chart shape from left to right	Vertical resizing	↕	Changes chart shape from top to bottom

Clues to Use

Changing the location of a chart

Suppose you have created an embedded chart that you decide would look better on a chart sheet. You can make this change without recreating the entire chart. To change the location of a selected chart, click Chart on the menu bar, then click Location. If the chart is embedded, click the As new sheet option button, then click OK. If the chart is on its own sheet, click the As object in option button, then click OK.

Editing a Chart

Once you've created a chart, it's easy to modify it. You can change data values in the worksheet, and the chart is automatically updated to reflect the new data. You can also change a data point in a chart, and the corresponding data values in the worksheet are automatically updated. You can also easily change the type of chart displayed by using the buttons on the Chart toolbar. You look over your worksheet and realize the data for the Kansas City store in November and December is incorrect. After you correct this data, Jim asks you to see how the same data looks using different chart types.

STEPS

TROUBLE

If you cannot see the chart and data together on your screen, click View on the menu bar, click Zoom, then click 75%.

1. **If necessary, scroll the worksheet so that you can see both the chart and row 8 containing the Kansas City sales figures, click the** November Kansas City data point, **then click the data point again**

   Handles surround the data point. You can click and drag these handles to modify the plotted data value.

2. **Drag the upper handle until the ScreenTip displays 21000**

   The value in cell F8 displays 21000.

3. **Click cell** G8, **type** 23000, **then click the** Enter button **on the formula bar**

   The Kansas City columns for November and December reflect the increased sales figures. See Figure D-8. The totals in column H and row 10 are also updated.

4. **Select the chart by clicking a blank area within the chart border, then click the** Chart Type list arrow **on the Chart toolbar**

   The Chart Type buttons appear on the Chart Type palette. Table D-3 describes the principal chart types available.

QUICK TIP

As you work with charts, experiment with different formats for your charts until you get just the right look.

5. **Click the** Bar Chart button **on the palette**

   The column chart changes to a bar chart. See Figure D-9. You look at the bar chart, take some notes, then decide to see if the large increase in sales would be better presented with a three-dimensional column chart.

6. **Click** , **then click the** 3-D Column Chart button **on the palette**

   A three-dimensional column chart appears. You notice that the three-dimensional column format is more crowded than the two-dimensional format, but it gives you a sense of volume.

QUICK TIP

The Chart Type button displays the last chart type selected.

7. **Click** , **then click the** Column Chart button **on the palette**

8. **Click the** Save button **on the Standard toolbar**

TABLE D-3: Commonly used chart type buttons

click to display a	click to display a	click to display a	click to display a
area chart	pie chart	3-D area chart	3-D pie chart
bar chart	(XY) scatter chart	3-D bar chart	3-D surface chart
column chart	doughnut chart	3-D column chart	3-D cylinder chart
line chart	radar chart	3-D line chart	3-D cone chart

FIGURE D-8: Worksheet with new data entered for Kansas City

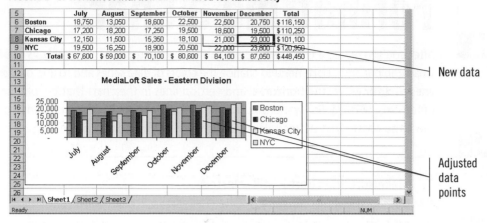

New data

Adjusted
data
points

FIGURE D-9: Bar chart

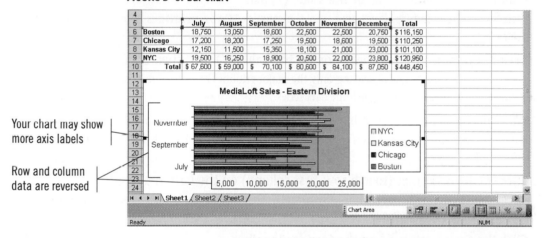

Your chart may show
more axis labels

Row and column
data are reversed

Clues to Use

Rotating a 3-D chart

In a three-dimensional chart, other data series in the same chart can sometimes obscure columns or bars. You can rotate the chart to obtain a better view. Click the chart, click the Corners object located at the tip of one of its axes, then drag the handle until a more pleasing view of the data series appears. See Figure D-10.

FIGURE D-10: 3-D chart rotated with improved view of data series

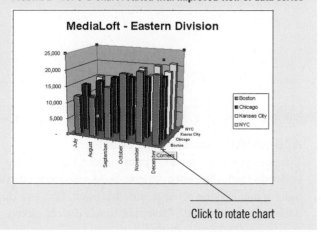

Click to rotate chart

Formatting a Chart

After you've created a chart using the Chart Wizard, you can easily modify its appearance. You can use the Chart toolbar and Chart menu to change the colors of data series and to add or eliminate a legend and gridlines. **Gridlines** are the horizontal and vertical lines in the chart that enable the eye to follow the value on an axis. Jim wants you to make some changes in the appearance of the chart. He wants to see if the chart looks better without gridlines, and he wants you to change the color of a data series.

STEPS

1. **Make sure the chart is still selected**

   Horizontal gridlines currently extend from the value axis tick marks across the chart's plot area.

2. **Click Chart on the menu bar, click Chart Options, click the Gridlines tab in the Chart Options dialog box, then click the Major Gridlines check box for the Value (Y) axis to remove the check mark**

   The gridlines disappear from the sample chart in the dialog box, as shown in Figure D-11.

3. **Click the Major gridlines check box for the Value (Y) axis to reselect it, then click the Minor gridlines check box for the Value (Y) axis**

   Both major and minor gridlines appear in the sample. **Minor gridlines** show the values between the tick marks.

4. **Click the Minor gridlines check box for the Value (Y) axis, then click OK**

   The minor gridlines disappear, leaving only the major gridlines on the value axis. You can change the color of the columns to better distinguish the data series.

5. **With the chart selected, double-click any light blue column in the NYC data series**

   Handles appear on all the columns in the NYC data series, and the Format Data Series dialog box opens, as shown in Figure D-12.

6. **Click the fuchsia color (fourth row, first column) on the Patterns tab, then click OK**

   All the columns for the series become fuchsia, and the legend changes to match the new color. Compare your formatted chart to Figure D-13.

7. **Click the Save button 🔲 on the Standard toolbar**

Clues to Use

Adding data labels to a chart

There are times when your audience might benefit by seeing data labels on a chart. These labels can indicate the series name, category name, and/or the value of one or more data points. Once your chart is selected, you can add this information to your chart by clicking

Chart on the menu bar, clicking Chart Options, then clicking the Data Labels tab in the Chart Options dialog box. You can also apply formatting to data labels, or delete individual data labels.

FIGURE D-11: Chart Options dialog box

Sample chart appears without gridlines

FIGURE D-12: Format Data Series dialog box

Sample of selected color

FIGURE D-13: Chart with formatted data series

Gridlines make it easy to follow axis values

New data series color

New color appears in legend

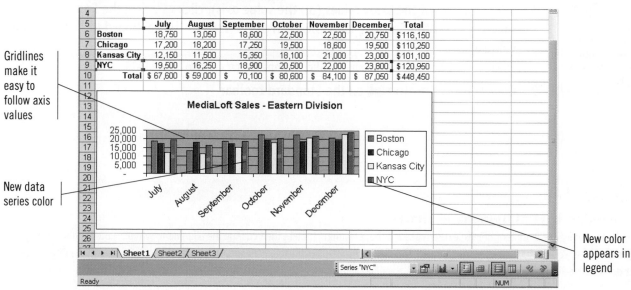

Excel 2003

Enhancing a Chart

There are many ways to enhance a chart to make it easier to read and understand. You can create titles for the x-axis and y-axis, add graphics, or add background color. You can even format the text you use in a chart. Many enhancements can be made using the Chart toolbar buttons. These buttons are listed in Table D-4. Jim wants you to improve the appearance of the chart by creating titles for the category axis and value axis and adding a drop shadow to the chart title.

STEPS

1. **Click a blank area of the chart to select the chart, click Chart on the menu bar, click Chart Options, click the Titles tab in the Chart Options dialog box, then type Months in the Category (X) axis text box**

   Descriptive text on the category axis helps readers understand the chart. The word "Months" appears below the month labels in the sample chart, as shown in Figure D-14.

> **QUICK TIP**
>
> To edit the text, position the pointer over the selected text box until it changes to I, click the text box, then edit the text.

2. **Type Sales (in $) in the Value (Y) axis text box, then click OK**

   A selected text box containing "Sales (in $)" appears rotated 90 degrees to the left of the value axis. Once the Chart Options dialog box is closed, you can move the value or title to a new position by clicking an edge of the object then dragging it.

3. **Press [Esc] on the keyboard to deselect the value axis title**

   Next you decide that a border with a drop shadow will enhance the chart title.

4. **Click the MediaLoft Sales – Eastern Division chart title to select it**

> **QUICK TIP**
>
> The Format button on the Chart toolbar opens a dialog box with the appropriate formatting options for the selected chart element. The ScreenTip for the button changes, depending on the selected object.

5. **Click the Format Chart Title button on the Chart toolbar to open the Format Chart Title dialog box, make sure the Patterns tab is selected, then click the Shadow check box to select it**

   A border with a drop shadow appears in the sample area.

6. **Click the Font tab in the Format Chart Title dialog box, click Times New Roman in the Font list, click Bold Italic in the Font style list, click OK, then press [Esc] on the keyboard to deselect the chart title**

   A border with a drop shadow appears around the chart title, and the chart title text is reformatted.

7. **Click any one of the months (on the category axis), click , click the Font tab in the Format Axis dialog box if necessary, click 8 in the Size list if necessary, then click OK**

   The size of the category axis text decreases, making more of the plot area visible.

> **QUICK TIP**
>
> You can also double-click the text on the value axis to open the Format Axis Titles dialog box.

8. **Click any one of the sales values (on the value axis), click , click the Font tab if necessary, click 8 in the Size list, click OK, then press [Esc] on the keyboard to deselect the value axis**

   The text on the value axis becomes smaller. Compare your chart to Figure D-15.

9. **Click the Save button on the Standard toolbar**

Clues to Use

Changing text alignment in charts

You can modify the alignment of axis text to make it fit better within the plot area. With a chart selected, double-click the axis text to be modified. The Format Axis dialog box opens. Click the Alignment tab, then change the alignment by typing the number of degrees in the Degrees text box, or by clicking a marker in the Degrees sample box. When you have made the desired changes, click OK.

FIGURE D-14: Sample chart with Category (X) axis text

Category axis title

FIGURE D-15: Enhanced chart

Drop shadow added

Value axis title

Resized axis labels

Category axis title

TABLE D-4: Chart enhancement buttons

button	use
	Displays the Format dialog box for the selected chart object
	Selects chart type (chart type on button changes to last chart type selected)
	Adds/deletes legend
	Creates a data table within the chart
	Charts data by row
	Charts data by column
	Angles selected text downward (clockwise)
	Angles selected text upward (counterclockwise)

Annotating and Drawing on a Chart

You can add arrows and text annotations to point out critical information in your charts. **Text annotations** are labels that you add to a chart to further describe your data. You can draw lines and arrows that point to the exact locations you want to emphasize. ▰▰▰▰ Jim wants you to add a text annotation and an arrow to highlight the October sales increase.

STEPS

1. **Make sure the chart is selected**

   To call attention to the Boston October sales increase, you can draw an arrow that points to the top of the Boston October data series with the annotation, "Due to ad campaign." With the chart selected, simply typing text in the formula bar creates annotation text.

2. **Type Due to ad campaign, then click the Enter button ✔ on the formula bar**

   As you type, the text appears in the formula bar. After you confirm the entry, the text appears in a selected text box on the chart.

3. **Point to an edge of the text box so that the pointer changes to ⁺ₖ**

4. **Drag the text box above the chart, as shown in Figure D-16, then release the mouse button**

   You can add an arrow to point to a specific area or item in a chart by using the Drawing toolbar.

5. **Click the Drawing button ⬚ on the Standard toolbar if necessary to display the Drawing toolbar**

   The Drawing toolbar appears below the worksheet.

6. **Click the Arrow button ⬂ on the Drawing toolbar, then move the pointer over the chart**

   The pointer changes to ╈, and the status bar displays "Click and drag to insert an AutoShape." When you draw an arrow, the point farthest from where you start has the arrowhead.

7. **Position ╈ under the t in the word "to" in the text box, press and hold the left mouse button, drag the line to the Boston column in the October sales series, then release the mouse button**

   An arrow appears, pointing to Boston October sales. The arrow is a selected object in the chart; you can resize, format, or delete it just like any other object. Compare your finished chart to Figure D-17.

8. **Click ⬚ to close the Drawing toolbar**

9. **Click the Save button ⬚ on the Standard toolbar**

Clues to Use

Adding an organizational chart or other diagram type

In addition to charts, annotations, and drawn objects, you can create a variety of diagrams. Diagram types include an Organization Chart, Cycle, Radial, Pyramid, Venn, or Target diagram. To insert a diagram, click Insert on the menu bar, then click Diagram. In the Diagram Gallery dialog box, click a diagram type, then click OK. The diagram appears on the worksheet as an embedded object with sizing handles, and the Diagram toolbar opens. You can edit placeholder text and use the Diagram toolbar buttons to insert or modify shapes, change the layout or diagram type, or select an AutoFormat. A selected diagram shape can be formatted using the Drawing toolbar buttons.

FIGURE D-16: Repositioning text annotation

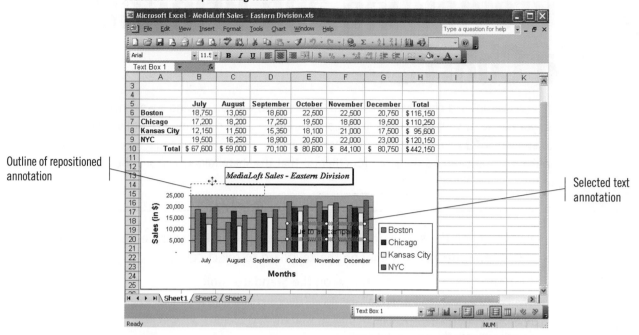

Outline of repositioned annotation

Selected text annotation

FIGURE D-17: Completed chart with text annotation and arrow

Repositioned text annotation

Arrow

Boston October sales

Drawing toolbar

Clues to Use

Exploding a pie slice

Just as an arrow can call attention to a data series, you can emphasize a pie slice by exploding, or pulling it away from, the pie chart. Once the pie chart is selected, click the pie to select it, click the desired slice to select only that slice, then drag the slice away from the pie, as shown in Figure D-18. After you change the chart type, you may need to adjust arrows within the chart.

FIGURE D-18: Exploded pie slice

Eastern Division - 6 Months Sales

$87,050 $67,600
          $59,000
$84,100
$80,600 $70,100

☐ July ■ August ☐ September ☐ October ■ November ■ December

Slice pulled from pie

Excel 2003

UNIT
D
Excel 2003

Previewing and Printing a Chart

After you complete a chart, you often need to print it. As with previewing a worksheet, previewing a chart lets you see what your chart looks like before you print it. You can print a chart by itself or as part of the worksheet. ▰▰▰▰▰ Jim wants a printed version of the chart for the annual meeting. He wants you to print the worksheet and the chart together, so that the shareholders can see the actual sales numbers for the Eastern Division stores.

STEPS

1. **Press [Esc] on the keyboard to deselect the arrow and the chart, enter your name in cell A35, then press [Ctrl][Home] on the keyboard to select cell A1**

2. **Click the Print Preview button 🔍 on the Standard toolbar**
   The Print Preview window opens. You decide the chart and data would fit better on the page if they were printed in **landscape** orientation—that is, with the text running the long way on the page. You use Page Setup to change the page orientation.

3. **Click Setup on the Print Preview toolbar to open the Page Setup dialog box, then click the Page tab, if necessary**

4. **Click the Landscape option button in the Orientation section, as shown in Figure D-19, then click OK**
   Because each page has a default left margin of 0.75", the chart and data will print too far over to the left of the page. You can change this setting using the Margins tab of the Page Setup dialog box.

5. **Click Setup on the Print Preview toolbar, click the Margins tab, click the Horizontally check box under Center on page, then click OK**
   The data and chart are positioned horizontally on the page. See Figure D-20.

6. **Click Print to display the Print dialog box, then click OK**
   The data and chart print, and you are returned to the worksheet. If you want, you can choose to preview (and print) only the chart.

7. **Select the chart, then click 🔍**
   The chart appears in the Print Preview window. If you wanted to, you could print the chart by clicking the Print button on the Print Preview toolbar.

8. **Click Close on the Print Preview toolbar**

9. **Click the Save button 🖫 on the Standard toolbar, close the workbook, then exit Excel**

FIGURE D-19: Page tab of the Page Setup dialog box

Landscape option
button selected

Depending on your
printer, your settings
might differ

FIGURE D-20: Chart and data ready to print

Centered
on page

Orientation
changed to
landscape

Chart and
data will
print on
one page

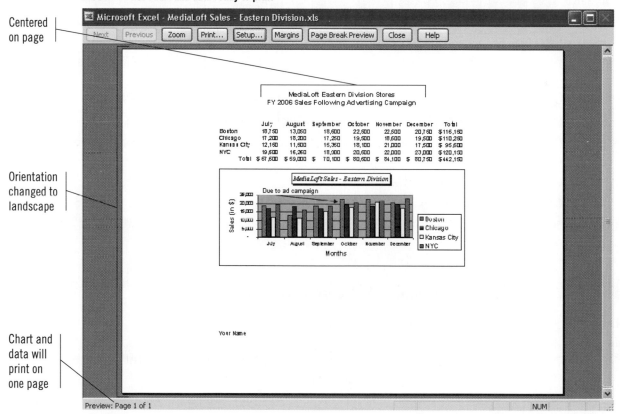

Clues to Use

Using the Page Setup dialog box for a chart

When a chart is selected, a different Page Setup dialog box opens than when neither the chart nor data is selected. The Center on Page options are not always available. To accurately position a chart on the page, you can click the Margins button on the Print Preview toolbar. Margin lines appear on the screen and show you exactly how the margins appear on the page. The exact placement appears in the status bar when you press and hold the mouse button on the margin line. You can drag the lines to the exact settings you want.

Practice

Label each element of the Excel chart shown in Figure D-21.

FIGURE D-21

Match each chart type with the statement that best describes it.

7. **Combination**   a. Shows how volume changes over time
8. **Column**   b. Compares data as parts of a whole
9. **Line**   c. Displays a column and line chart using different scales of measurement
10. **Area**   d. Compares trends over even time intervals
11. **Pie**   e. Compares data over time—the Excel default

Select the best answer from the list of choices.

12. **Which pointer is used to resize a chart object?**

    a. I

    b. ↘

    c. ↔↕

    d. +

13. **The object in a chart that identifies patterns used for each data series is a:**

    a. Data point.

    b. Plot.

    c. Legend.

    d. Range.

14. **The orientation of a page whose dimensions are 11" wide by 8 ½" tall is:**

    a. Portrait.

    b. Longways.

    c. Landscape.

    d. Sideways.

15. **What is the term for a row or column on a chart?**

    a. Range address

    b. Axis title

    c. Chart orientation

    d. Data series

16. **In a 2-D chart, the category axis is the:**

    a. X-axis.

    b. Z-axis.

    c. D-axis.

    d. Y-axis.

17. **In a 2-D chart, the value axis is the:**

    a. X-axis.

    b. Y-axis.

    c. D-axis.

    d. Z-axis.

▼ SKILLS REVIEW

1. **Plan and design a chart.**

   a. Start Excel, open the Data File EX D-2.xls from the drive and folder where your Data Files are stored, then save it as **MediaLoft Vancouver Software Usage**.

   b. Sketch the type of chart you would use to plot this data.

   c. In what chart type is the y-axis referred to as the z-axis?

   d. What term is used to describe the visual representation of each data point?

2. **Create a chart.**

   a. Select the range containing the data and headings.

   b. Start the Chart Wizard.

   c. In the Chart Wizard, select a clustered column chart, then verify that the series are in rows, add the chart title **Software Usage by Department**, and make the chart an object on the worksheet.

   d. After the chart appears, save your work.

3. **Move and resize a chart.**

   a. Make sure the chart is still selected.

   b. Move the chart beneath the data.

   c. Resize the chart so it extends to column J.

   d. Use the Legend tab in the Chart Options dialog box to move the legend below the charted data.

   e. Resize the chart so the bottom is at the top of row 25.

   f. Save your work.

4. **Edit a chart.**

   a. Change the value in cell B3 to 6. Notice the change in the chart.

   b. Select the chart.

   c. Use the Chart Type list arrow to change the chart to a 3-D Column Chart.

   d. Rotate the chart to move the data.

   e. Change the chart back to a column chart.

   f. Save your work.

5. **Format a chart.**

   a. Make sure the chart is still selected.

   b. Use the Chart Options dialog box to turn off the displayed gridlines.

   c. Change the font used in the Category and Value labels to Times New Roman.

   d. Turn on the major gridlines for the value axis.

   e. Change the chart title's font to Times New Roman, with a font size of 18.

   f. Save your work.

6. **Enhance a chart.**

   a. Make sure the chart is selected, then select the Titles tab in the Chart Options dialog box.

   b. Enter Software as the x-axis title.

   c. Enter Users as the y-axis title.

   d. Change Production in the legend to Art. (*Hint*: Change the text entry in the worksheet.)

   e. Add a drop shadow to the chart title.

   f. Save your work.

7. **Annotate and draw on a chart.**

   a. Make sure the chart is selected, then create the text annotation Needs More Users.

   b. Position the text annotation beneath the chart title.

   c. Below the text annotation, use the Drawing toolbar to create an arrow that points to the area containing the Access data.

   d. Compare your work to Figure D-22.

   e. Save your work.

FIGURE D-22

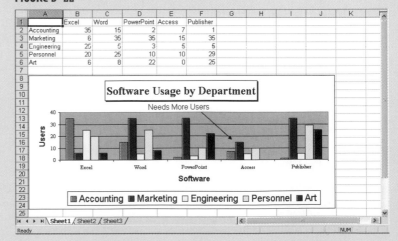

8. Preview and print a chart.

    a. In the worksheet, enter your name in cell A30.

    b. Preview the chart and data.

    c. Change the page orientation to landscape.

    d. Center the page contents horizontally and vertically on the page.

    e. Print the data and chart from the Print Preview window.

    f. Save your work.

    g. Preview only the chart, then print it.

    h. Close the workbook, then exit Excel.

▼ INDEPENDENT CHALLENGE 1

You are the operations manager for the Springfield Theater Group in Oregon. Each year the group applies to various state and federal agencies for matching funds. For this year's funding proposal, you need to create charts to document the number of productions in previous years.

    a. Sketch a sample worksheet on a piece of paper describing how you will create the charts. Which type of chart is best suited for the information you need to display? What kind of chart enhancements do you want to use? Will a 3-D effect make your chart easier to understand?

    b. Start Excel, open the Data File EX D-3.xls, then save it as **Springfield Theater Group** in the drive and folder where your Data Files are stored.

    c. Create a column chart for the data, accepting all Chart Wizard defaults.

    d. Change at least one of the colors used in a data series.

    e. Create at least two additional charts for the same data to show how different chart types display the same data. Each of these charts should be on its own chart sheet in the workbook.

    f. After creating the charts, make the appropriate enhancements. Include chart titles, legends, and value and category axis titles, using the suggestions in Table D-5.

    g. Add data labels.

    h. Enter your name in a worksheet cell.

    i. Save your work. Before printing, preview the workbook so you know what the charts look like. Adjust any items as necessary.

    j. Print the worksheet (charts and data).

    k. Close the workbook, then exit Excel.

TABLE D-5

suggested chart enhancements	
Title	Types and Number of Plays
Legend	Year 1, Year 2, Year 3, Year 4
Value axis title	Number of Plays
Category axis title	Play Types

Excel 2003

▼ INDEPENDENT CHALLENGE 2

Beautiful You, a small beauty salon, has been using Excel for several months. One of your responsibilities at the Beautiful You salon is to re-create the company's records using Excel. Another is to convince the current staff that Excel can help them make daily operating decisions more easily and efficiently. To do this, you've decided to create charts using the previous year's operating expenses, including rent, utilities, and payroll. The manager will use these charts at the next monthly meeting.

a. Decide which data in the worksheet should be charted. Sketch two sample charts. What type of charts are best suited for the information you need to show? What kind of chart enhancements are necessary?

b. Start Excel, open the Data File EX D-4.xls from the drive and folder where your Data Files are stored, then save it as **BY Expense Charts**.

c. Create a column chart on the worksheet, containing the expense data for all four quarters.

d. Using the same data, create an area chart and one additional chart using any other appropriate chart type. (*Hint*: Move each chart to a new location on the worksheet, then deselect it before using the Wizard to create the next one.)

e. Add annotated text and arrows to the column chart that highlight any important data or trends.

f. In one chart, change the color of a data series, then in another chart, use black-and-white patterns only. (*Hint*: Use the Fill Effects button in the Format Data Series dialog box. Then display the Patterns tab. Adjust the Foreground color to black and the Background color to white, then select a pattern.)

g. Enter your name in a worksheet cell.

h. Save your work. Before printing, preview each chart so you know what the charts look like. Adjust any items as needed.

i. Print the charts.

j. Close the workbook, then exit Excel.

▼ INDEPENDENT CHALLENGE 3

You are working as an account representative at the Bright Light Ad Agency. You have been examining the expenses charged to clients of the firm. The Board of Directors wants to examine certain advertising expenses and has asked you to prepare charts that can be used in this evaluation.

a. Start Excel, open the Data File EX D-5.xls from the drive and folder where your Data Files are stored, then save it as **Bright Light**.

b. Decide what types of charts would be best suited for the data in the range A16:B24. Sketch three sample charts. What kind of chart enhancements are necessary?

c. Use the Chart Wizard to create at least three different types of charts that show the distribution of advertising expenses. (*Hint*: Move each chart to a new location on the worksheet, then deselect it before using the Wizard to create the next one.) One of the charts should be a 3-D pie chart.

d. Add annotated text and arrows highlighting important data, such as the largest expense.

e. Change the color of at least one data series.

f. Add chart titles and category and value axis titles. Format the titles with a font of your choice. Place a drop shadow around the chart title.

Advanced Challenge Exercise

- Explode a slice from the 3-D pie chart.
- Add a data label to the exploded pie slice.
- Change the alignment of labels on an axis.
- Modify the scale of the value axis in one of the charts. (*Hint*: Double-click the gridlines to open the Format Gridlines dialog box, then click the Scale tab.)

g. Enter your name in a worksheet cell.

h. Save your work. Before printing, preview the file so you know what the charts look like. Adjust any items as needed. Be sure the chart is placed appropriately on the page.

i. Print the charts, close the workbook, then exit Excel.

▼ INDEPENDENT CHALLENGE 4

Your company, Film Distribution, is headquartered in Montreal, and is considering opening a new office in the United States. Your supervisor would like you to begin investigating possible locations. You can use the Web to find and compare median pay scales in specific cities to see how relocating will affect the standard of living for those employees who move to the new office.

a. Start Excel, open a new workbook, then save it as **New Location Analysis** in the drive and folder where your Data Files are located.

b. Use your favorite search engine to find your own information sources on salary calculators, or cost-of-living calculators.

c. Determine the median incomes for Seattle, San Francisco, Dallas, Salt Lake City, Memphis, and Boston. Record this data on a sheet named **Median Income** in your workbook. See Table D-6 below for suggested data layout.

d. Format the data so it looks attractive and professional.

e. Create any type of column chart, with the data series in columns, on the same worksheet as the data. Include a descriptive title.

f. Remove the major gridlines in the Median Income chart.

g. On a blank worksheet in the current workbook, determine how much an employee would need to earn in Seattle, San Francisco, Dallas, Memphis, and Boston to maintain the same standard of living as if the company chose to relocate to Salt Lake City and pay $75,000. Name the sheet **Standard of Living**.

TABLE D-6

location	income
Seattle	
San Francisco	
Dallas	
Salt Lake City	
Memphis	
Boston	

h. Format the data so it looks attractive and professional.

i. Create a 3-D column chart on the same worksheet as the data. Include a descriptive title.

j. Change the color of the data series in the Standard of Living chart to bright green.

Advanced Challenge Exercise

■ Format the value axis in your chart(s) so that the salary income displays a 1000 separator (comma), but no dollar sign or decimal places.

■ Rotate the chart so you get a different view of the data.

■ Change the alignment of the category axis labels.

k. Do not display the legends in your chart(s).

l. Enter your name in a cell in your worksheet(s).

m. Save the workbook. Preview the chart(s) and change margins as necessary.

n. Print your worksheet(s), including the data and chart(s), making setup modifications as necessary.

o. Close the workbook, then exit Excel.

▼ VISUAL WORKSHOP

Modify a worksheet, using the skills you learned in this unit and using Figure D-23 for reference. Open the Data File EX D-6.xls from the drive and folder where your Data Files are stored, then save it as **Quarterly Advertising Budget**. Create the chart, then change the chart to reflect Figure D-23. Enter your name in cell A13, save, preview, then print your results.

FIGURE D-23

Working with Formulas and Functions

OBJECTIVES

Create a formula with several operators
Use names in a formula
Generate multiple totals with AutoSum
Use dates in calculations
Build a conditional formula with the IF function
Use statistical functions
Calculate payments with the PMT function
Display and print formula contents

If you have a SAM user profile, you may have access to hands-on instruction, practice, and assessment of the skills covered in this unit. Log in to your SAM account and go to your assignments page to see what your instructor has assigned.

Without formulas, Excel would simply be an electronic grid with text and numbers. Used with formulas, Excel becomes a powerful data analysis tool. As you learn how to analyze data using different types of formulas, including those containing functions, you will discover more ways to use Excel. In this unit, you will gain a further understanding of Excel formulas and learn how to use several Excel functions. ▰▰▱ Top management at MediaLoft has asked marketing director Jim Fernandez to analyze various company data. To do this, Jim creates several worksheets that require formulas and functions. Because management is considering raising salaries for store managers, Jim has asked you to create a report that compares the payroll deductions and net pay for store managers before and after a proposed raise.

Creating a Formula with Several Operators

You can create formulas that contain a combination of cell references (for example, Z100 or B2), operators (for example, * for multiplication or – for subtraction), and values (for example, 99 or 1.56). Formulas can also contain functions. You have used AutoSum to insert the SUM function into a cell. You can also create a single formula that performs several calculations. If you enter a formula with more than one operator, Excel performs the calculations in a particular sequence based on algebraic rules, called the **order of precedence** (also called the order of operations); that is, Excel performs the operation(s) within parentheses first, then calculates exponents, then any multiplication and division from left to right. Finally, it calculates addition and subtraction, from left to right. See Table E-1 for examples. ▰▰▰▰ Jim has received the gross pay and deductions for the monthly payroll and needs to complete his analysis. He has also preformatted, with the Comma style, any cells that are to contain values. He asks you to enter a formula for net pay that subtracts the payroll deductions from gross pay.

STEPS

QUICK TIP
You can learn more about the possible errors that Excel has flagged by clicking the cell, clicking the list arrow that appears, then choosing an option.

1. **Start Excel if necessary, open the Data File EX E-1.xls from the drive and folder where your Data Files are stored, then save it as Company Data**

   The green triangles in the cells indicate that the formulas differ from the surrounding formulas. In this case, the formulas are correct, so you can ignore the triangles. The first part of the net pay formula should go in cell B11.

2. **Click Edit on the menu bar, click Go To, type B11 in the Reference box, then click OK**

   Cell B11 is now the active cell. The Go To command is especially useful when you want to select a cell in a large worksheet.

3. **Type =, click cell B6, type –, then click the Insert Function button 𝑓x on the formula bar to open the Insert Function dialog box**

   You type the equal sign (=) to indicate that a formula follows. B6 references the cell containing the gross pay, and the minus sign (–) indicates that the next entry, a sum, is subtracted from cell B6. The Insert Function dialog box allows you to choose from a list of available functions or search for a specific function. See Figure E-1.

TROUBLE
If you make a mistake while building a formula, press [Esc] and begin again.

4. **Type sum in the Search for a function text box, click Go, click SUM in the Select a function list, then click OK**

   B6:B10 appears in the Number1 text box. You want to sum the range B7:B10.

QUICK TIP
Instead of using the Collapse Dialog Box and the Redisplay Dialog Box buttons, you can drag the dialog box out of the way and select the desired range on the worksheet to insert it in the formula.

5. **With the Number1 argument selected in the Function Arguments dialog box, click the Number1 Collapse Dialog Box button ▦, select the range B7:B10 in the worksheet, click the Redisplay Dialog Box button ▦, then click OK**

   Collapsing the dialog box allows you to enter the range by selecting it. The net pay for Payroll Period 1 appears in cell B11.

6. **Copy the formula in cell B11 into cells C11:F11, then press [Ctrl][Home] to return to cell A1**

   The net pay for each column appears in row 11. See Figure E-2.

7. **Save the workbook**

FIGURE E-1: Insert Function dialog box

Type a function description

Click to start a function search

Your function listing may be different

Click to select the highlighted function

FIGURE E-2: Worksheet with copied formulas

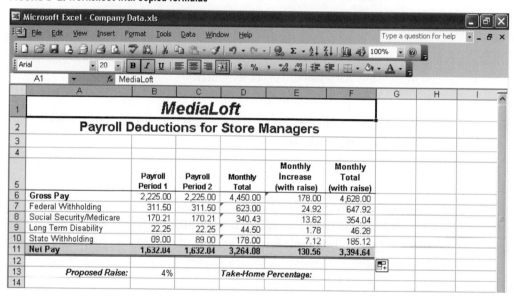

TABLE E-1: Sample formulas using parentheses and several operators

formula	order of precedence	calculated result
=10–20/10–5	Divide 20 by 10; subtract the result from 10, then subtract 5	3
=(10–20)/10–5	Subtract 20 from 10; divide that by 10; then subtract 5	–6
=(10*2)*(10+2)	Multiply 10 by 2; add 10 to 2; then multiply the results	240

Clues to Use

Using Paste Special

You can use the Paste Special command to enter formulas and values quickly or even to perform quick calculations. Click the cell(s) containing the formula or value you want to copy, click the Copy button on the Standard toolbar, then right-click the cell where you want the result to appear. In the shortcut menu, click Paste Special, choose the feature you want to paste, then click OK.

Using names in a Formula

To reduce errors and make your worksheet easier to follow, you can assign names to cells and ranges. You can also use names in formulas to make formulas easier to build. For example, the formula Revenue-Cost is much easier to understand than the formula A2-D3. When used in formulas, names become absolute cell references by default. Names can use uppercase or lowercase letters as well as digits. After you name a cell or range, you can use the name on any sheet in the workbook. If you move a named cell or range, its name moves with it. Jim wants you to include a formula that calculates the percentage of monthly gross pay that the managers would actually take home (their net pay) if they received a 4% raise. You decide to name the cells that you will use in the calculation.

STEPS

QUICK TIP

You can also assign names to ranges of cells. Select the range, click the name box, then type in the range name. You can also name a range by pointing to Name on the Insert menu, then clicking Define and typing the name.

1. **Click cell F6, click the name box on the formula bar to select the active cell reference, type Gross_with_Raise, then press [Enter]**

   The name assigned to cell F6, Gross_with_Raise, appears in the name box. Note that you must type underscores instead of spaces between words. Cell F6 is now named Gross_with_Raise to refer to the monthly gross pay amount that includes the 4% raise. The name box displays as much of the name as fits (Gross_with_…). The total net pay cell needs a name.

2. **Click cell F11, click the name box, type Net_with_Raise, then press [Enter]**

   The new formula uses names instead of cell references.

QUICK TIP

You can use the Label Ranges dialog box (Insert menu, Name submenu, Label command) to designate existing column or row headings as labels. Then instead of using cell references for the column or row in formulas, you can use the labels.

3. **Click cell F13, type =, click Insert on the menu bar, point to Name, click Paste, click Net_with_Raise, then click OK**

   The name is inserted and the color of the name matches the outline around the cell reference.

4. **Type /, click Insert on the menu bar, point to Name, click Paste, click Gross_with_Raise, click OK, then click the Enter button ✓ on the formula bar**

   The formula appears in the formula bar and the result, 0.7335, appears in the cell. Cell F13 needs to be formatted in Percent style.

QUICK TIP

To replace cell references in existing formulas with the corresponding names you have added, click Insert on the menu bar, point to Name, click Apply, click the name or names, then click OK.

5. **Select cell F13 if necessary, click Format on the menu bar, click Style, click the Style name list arrow, click Percent, then click OK**

   The result shown in cell F13, 73%, is rounded to the nearest whole percent, as shown in Figure E-3. A **style** is a combination of formatting characteristics, such as bold, italic, and zero decimal places. You can use the Style dialog box instead of the Formatting toolbar to apply styles.

6. **Enter your name in cell A20, save the workbook, then preview and print the worksheet**

Clues to Use

Defining and removing styles

To define your own style (such as bold, italic, 14 point numbers with commas and zero decimal places), select a cell, format it using the Formatting toolbar, open the Style dialog box and type a name for your style, then click Add. Later, you can apply all of your formatting characteristics by applying your new style from the Style dialog box. You can also use the Style dialog box to remove styles by selecting the cell that has a style and then selecting Normal in the Style name list.

FIGURE E-3: Worksheet formula that includes cell names

Name box

Formula with cell names

Cell named Gross_with_Raise

Cell named Net_with_Raise

Result of calculation

Clues to Use

Producing a list of names

You might want to verify the names you have assigned in a workbook and the cells they reference. To paste a list of names in a workbook, select a blank cell that has several blank cells beside and beneath it. Click Insert on the menu bar, point to Name, then click Paste. In the Paste Name dialog box, click Paste List. Excel produces a list of names that includes the sheet name followed by an exclamation point and the cell or range the name identifies. See Figure E-4.

FIGURE E-4: Worksheet with pasted list of names

Pasted list of names in workbook

Location of named cell

Excel 2003

Generating Multiple Totals with AutoSum

In most cases, the result of a function is a value derived from a single calculation. You have used AutoSum to produce a total of a single range of numbers; you can also use it to total multiple ranges. If you include blank cells to the right or at the bottom of a selected range, AutoSum generates several totals and enters the results in the blank cells. You can also use AutoSum to generate grand totals of worksheet subtotals. ▰▰▰▰▰ Maria Abbott, MediaLoft's general sales manager, has given Jim a worksheet summarizing store sales. He asks you to complete the worksheet totals.

STEPS

TROUBLE

If you select the wrong combination of cells, click a single cell and begin again.

1. **Click the Sales sheet tab to make the Sales sheet active, select the range B5:E9, press and hold [Ctrl], then select the range B11:E15**

   To select nonadjacent cells, you must press and hold [Ctrl] while selecting the additional cells. Compare your selections with Figure E-6. Jim would like totals to appear in the last line of each selection.

2. **Click the AutoSum button Σ on the Standard toolbar**

   When the selected range you want to sum (B5:E9 and B11:E15, in this example) includes a blank cell with data values above it, AutoSum enters the total in the blank cell.

3. **Select the range B5:F17, then click Σ**

   Although Excel generates totals when you click the AutoSum button, it is a good idea to check the results.

QUICK TIP

Excel uses commas to separate multiple arguments in all functions, not just in SUM.

4. **Click cell B17**

   The formula bar reads =SUM(B15,B9). In this case, Excel ignores the data values and it totals only the sums. See Figure E-7. When generating grand totals, Excel separates the cell references with a comma.

5. **Enter your name in cell A20, save the workbook, then preview and print the worksheet**

Clues to Use

Quick calculations with AutoCalculate

To view a total quickly without entering a formula, just select the range you want to sum. The answer appears in the status bar next to SUM=. You also can perform other quick calculations, such as averaging or finding the minimum value in a selection: right-click in the status bar, and select from the list of function names. The option you select remains in effect and in the status bar until you make another selection. See Figure E-5.

FIGURE E-5: Using AutoCalculate

List of AutoCalculate options

AutoCalculate area

Sum of current selection

FIGURE E-6: Selecting nonadjacent ranges using [Ctrl]

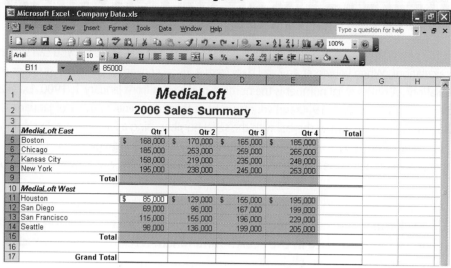

FIGURE E-7: Completed worksheet

Comma separates multiple arguments

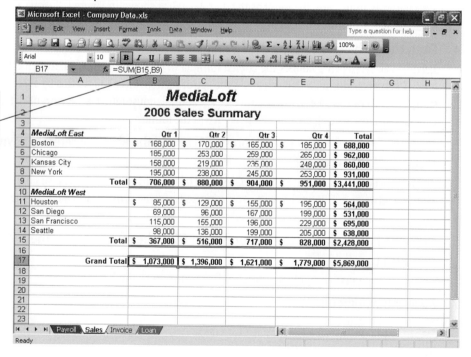

Using Dates in Calculations

If you enter dates in a worksheet in a format that Excel recognizes as a date, you can sort them and perform date calculations. When you enter an Excel date format, Excel converts it to a serial number so it can be used in calculations. A date's serial number is the number of days it is from January 1, 1900. Excel assigns the serial number of "1" to January 1, 1900 and counts up from there; the serial number of January 1, 2006, for example, is 38,718. When you format the cell with the serial number using a Date format, Excel displays the serial number as a date. Jim wants you to calculate the due date and age of each invoice on his worksheet. He reminds you to enter the worksheet dates in a format that Excel recognizes, so you can use date calculations.

STEPS

1. **Click the** Invoice sheet tab, **click cell** C4, **click the** Insert Function button 𝑓ₓ **on the formula bar, type** date **in the Search for a function text box, click** Go, **click** DATE **in the Select a function list, then click** OK

   Your calculations need to be based on a current date of 4/1/06.

TROUBLE

If the year appears with four digits instead of two, your system administrator may have set a four-digit year display. You can continue with the lesson.

2. **Enter** 2006 **in the Year text box, enter** 4 **in the Month text box, enter** 1 **in the Day text box, then click** OK

   The Date function uses the format DATE(year, month, day). The date appears in cell C4 as 4/1/06. Your formula in cell E7 should calculate the invoice due date, which is 30 days from the invoice date. The formula adds 30 days to the invoice date.

3. **Click cell** E7, **type** =, **click cell** B7, **type** +30, **then click the** Enter button ✓ **on the formula bar**

   Excel calculates the result by converting the 3/2/06 invoice date to a serial date number, adding 30 to it, then automatically formatting the result as the date 4/1/06, as shown in Figure E-8. You can use the same formula to calculate the due dates of the other invoices.

QUICK TIP

You can also perform time calculations in Excel. For example, you can enter an employee's starting and ending time, then calculate how long he or she worked. You must enter time in an Excel time format.

4. **Drag the fill handle to copy the formula in cell E7 into cells E8:E13**

   Relative cell referencing adjusts the copied formula to contain the appropriate cell references. Now you are ready to enter the formula that calculates the age of each invoice. You do this by subtracting the invoice date from the current date. Because each invoice age formula must refer to the current date, you must make cell C4, the current date cell, an absolute reference in the formula.

5. **Click cell** F7, **type** =, **click cell** C4, **press** [F4] **to add the absolute reference symbols ($), type** –, **click cell** B7, **then click** ✓

   The formula bar displays the formula $C$4–B7. The numerical result, 30, appears in cell F7 because there are 30 days between 3/2/06 and 4/1/06. You can use the same formula to calculate the age of the remaining invoices.

QUICK TIP

You can also insert the current date into a cell by using the TODAY() function. The NOW() function inserts the current date and time into a cell. If you leave the argument area within its parentheses blank, it automatically displays today's date.

6. **Drag the fill handle to copy the formula in F7 to the range** F8:F13, **then press** [Ctrl][Home] **to return to cell A1**

   The age of each invoice appears in column F, as shown in Figure E-9.

7. **Save the workbook**

FIGURE E-8: Worksheet with calculated invoice due date

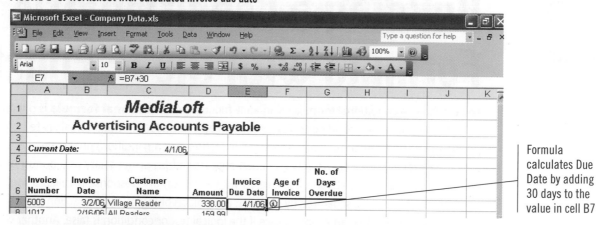

Formula calculates Due Date by adding 30 days to the value in cell B7

FIGURE E-9: Worksheet with copied formulas

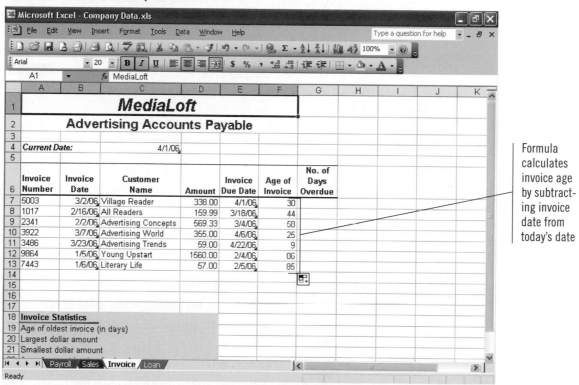

Formula calculates invoice age by subtracting invoice date from today's date

Clues to Use

Applying and creating custom number and date formats

When you use numbers and dates in worksheets or calculations, you can apply built-in Excel formats or create your own. To apply number formats, click Format on the menu bar, click Cells, then if necessary click the Number tab. In the Category list, click a category, then click the exact format in the list or scroll box to the right. To create a custom format, click Custom in the category list, then click a format that resembles the one you want. For example the value $3,789 uses the number format $#,### where # represents positive numbers. In the Type box, edit the symbols until they represent the format you want, then click OK. See Figure E-10.

FIGURE E-10: Custom formats on the Number tab in the Format Cells dialog box

Semicolons separate the codes that define the formats for positive numbers, negative numbers, zero values, and text

Custom formats

Edit these symbol sequences to customize the format selected below

Custom formats category

Building a Conditional Formula with the IF Function

You can build a conditional formula using an IF function. A **conditional formula** is one that makes calculations based on stated conditions. For example, you can build a formula to calculate bonuses based on a person's performance rating. If a person is rated a 5 (the stated condition) on a scale of 1 to 5, with 5 being the highest rating, he or she receives an additional 10% of his or her salary as a bonus; otherwise, there is no bonus. A condition that can be answered with a true or false response is called a **logical test**. The IF function has three parts, separated by commas: a condition or logical test, an action to take if the logical test or condition is true, then an action to take if the logical test or condition is false. Another way of expressing this is: IF(test_cond,do_this,else_this). Translated into an Excel IF function, the formula to calculate bonuses would look something like this: IF(Rating=5,Salary*0.10,0). The translation would be: If the rating equals 5, multiply the salary by 0.10 (the decimal equivalent of 10%), then place the result in the selected cell; if the rating does not equal 5, place a 0 in the cell. When entering the logical test portion of an IF statement, you typically use some combination of the comparison operators listed in Table E-2. ████ You are almost finished with the invoice worksheet. To complete it, you need to use an IF function that calculates the number of days each invoice is overdue.

STEPS

1. **Click cell G7, click the Insert Function button *fx* on the formula bar, enter conditional in the Search for a function text box, click Go, click IF in the Select a function list box, then click OK**

   You want the function to calculate the number of days overdue as follows: if the age of the invoice is greater than 30, calculate the days overdue (Age of Invoice – 30), and place the result in cell G7; otherwise, place a 0 (zero) in the cell.

2. **Enter F7>30 in the Logical_test text box**

   The symbol (>) represents "greater than." So far, the formula reads: if Age of Invoice is greater than 30 (in other words, if the invoice is overdue). The next part of the function tells Excel the action to take if the invoice is over 30 days old.

3. **Enter F7–30 in the Value_if_true text box**

   This part of the formula is what you want Excel to do if the logical test is true (that is, if the age of the invoice is over 30). Continuing the translation of the formula, this part means: take the Age of Invoice value and subtract 30. The last part of the formula tells Excel the action to take if the logical test is false (that is, if the age of the invoice is 30 days or less).

4. **Enter 0 in the Value_if_false text box, then click OK**

   The function is complete, and the result, 0 (the number of days overdue), appears in cell G7. See Figure E-11.

5. **Copy the formula in cell G7 into cells G8:G13, then press [Ctrl][Home] to return to cell A1**

   Compare your results with Figure E-12.

6. **Save the workbook**

TABLE E-2: Comparison operators

operator	meaning	operator	meaning
<	Less than	<=	Less than or equal to
>	Greater than	>=	Greater than or equal to
=	Equal to	<>	Not equal to

FIGURE E-11: Worksheet with IF function

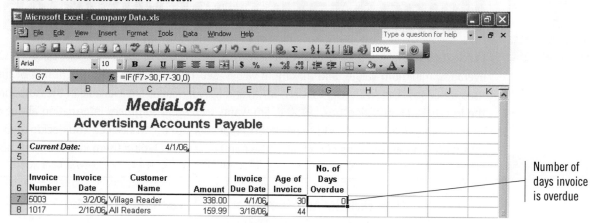

Number of days invoice is overdue

FIGURE E-12: Completed worksheet

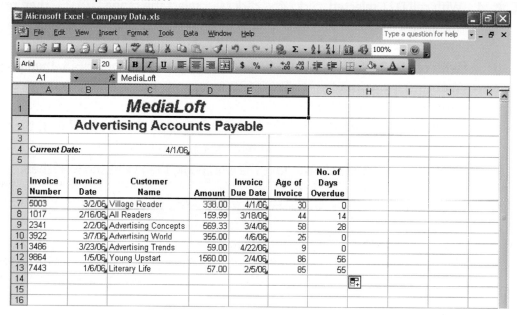

Clues to Use

Correcting circular references

A cell with a circular reference contains a formula that refers to its own cell location. If you accidentally enter a formula with a circular reference, a warning box opens alerting you to the problem. Click OK to display the Circular Reference toolbar or HELP to open a Help window explaining how to find the circular reference. In simple formulas, a circular reference is easy to spot. To correct it, edit the formula to remove any reference to the cell where the formula is located.

Using Statistical Functions

Excel offers several hundred worksheet functions. A small group of these functions calculate statistics such as averages, minimum values, and maximum values. See Table E-3 for a brief description of these commonly used functions. The AVERAGE, COUNT, MAX, and MIN functions are available in the AutoSum list as well as the Insert Function dialog box. Jim wants to present summary information about open accounts payable, and he asks you to add some statistical functions to the worksheet. You decide to use the AutoSum list to insert these functions because it is faster and easier than typing them into the worksheet.

STEPS

1. **Click cell D19, click the** AutoSum list arrow Σ ▾ **and then click** Max

   The invoice age information is in cells F7:F13.

2. **Select the range** F7:F13, **then press** [Enter]

   The age of the oldest invoice (or maximum value in range F7:F13) is 86 days, as shown in Figure E-13. Jim needs to know the largest dollar amount among the outstanding invoices.

3. **With cell D20 selected, click** Σ ▾ **, click** Max, **select the range** D7:D13, **then press** [Enter]

   The largest outstanding invoice, for 1560.00, is shown in cell D20. The MIN function finds the smallest dollar amount and the age of the newest invoice.

   QUICK TIP
   You can cut, copy, and paste functions from one worksheet area to another or from one workbook to another.

4. **With cell D21 selected, click** Σ ▾ **, click** Min, **select the range** D7:D13, **then press** [Enter]

   The smallest dollar amount owed is 57.00, as shown in cell D21. Jim wants to know the age of the newest invoice.

5. **With cell D22 selected, click** Σ ▾ **, click** Min, **select the range** F7:F13, **then press** [Enter]

   The newest invoice is 9 days old. The COUNT function calculates the number of invoices by counting the number of entries in column A.

6. **With cell D23 selected, click** Σ ▾ **, click** COUNT, **select the range** A7:A13, **then press** [Enter]

   Cell D23 confirms that there are seven invoices. Compare your worksheet with Figure E-14.

7. **Enter your name in cell A26, save the workbook, then print the worksheet**

TABLE E-3: Commonly used statistical functions

function	worksheet action	function	worksheet action
AVERAGE	Calculates an average value	MAX	Finds the largest value
COUNT	Counts cells that contain numbers	MIN	Finds the smallest value
COUNTA	Counts cells that contain nonblank entries	MEDIAN	Finds the middle value

FIGURE E-13: Worksheet with age of oldest invoice

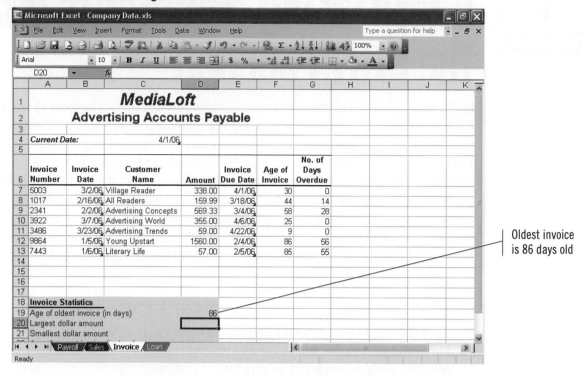

Oldest invoice is 86 days old

FIGURE E-14: Worksheet with invoice statistics

Number of invoices in A7:A13

Clues to Use

Using the COUNTA function

The COUNT function counts the number of cells that contain numeric data. If the cell entries that you are trying to count contain nonnumerical data (such as invoice numbers with text entries), the COUNT function does not work and displays a count of zero. There is another function, COUNTA, that counts the number of cells that are not empty and therefore can be used to count the number of entries that contain text.

Calculating Payments with the PMT Function

PMT is a financial function that calculates the periodic payment amount for money borrowed. For example, if you want to borrow money to buy a car, and you know the principal amount, interest rate, and loan term, the PMT function can calculate your monthly payment. Say you want to borrow $15,000 at 8.5% interest and pay the loan off in five years. The Excel PMT function can tell you that your monthly payment will be $307.75 The parts of the PMT function are: PMT(rate, nper, pv, fv, type). See Figure E-15 for an illustration of a PMT function that calculates the monthly payment in the car loan example. ▄▄▄▄ For several months, MediaLoft management has been discussing the expansion of the San Diego store. Jim has obtained quotes from three different lenders on borrowing $29,000 to begin the expansion. He obtained loan quotes from a commercial bank, a venture capitalist, and an investment banker. He wants you to summarize the information, using the Excel PMT function.

STEPS

1. **Click the Loan sheet tab, click cell E5, click the Insert Function button 𝑓ₓ on the formula bar, enter pmt in the Search for a function text box, click Go, click PMT in the Select a function list if necessary, then click OK**

2. **Move the Function Arguments dialog box so you can see row 5 of the worksheet; with the cursor in the Rate text box, click cell C5 on the worksheet, type /12, then press [Tab]**
   You must divide the annual interest by 12 because you are calculating monthly, not annual, payments.

> **QUICK TIP**
> You must be consistent about the units you use for rate and nper. If you express nper as the number of monthly payments, then you must express the interest rate as a monthly rate.

3. **With the cursor in the Nper text box, click cell D5; click the Pv text box, click cell B5, then click OK**
   The FV and Type are optional arguments. Note that the payment of ($581.10) in cell E5 appears in red, indicating that it is a negative amount. Excel displays the result of a PMT function as a negative value to reflect the negative cash flow the loan represents to the borrower. To show the monthly payment as a positive number, you place a minus sign in front of the Pv cell reference in the function.

4. **Edit cell E5 so it reads =PMT(C5/12,D5,–B5), then click the Enter button ✓**
   A positive value of $581.10 now appears in cell E5. See Figure E-16. You can use the same formula to generate the monthly payments for the other loans.

5. **With cell E5 selected, drag the fill handle to fill the range E6:E7**
   A monthly payment of $895.44 for the venture capitalist loan appears in cell E6. A monthly payment of $1,296.43 for the investment banker loan appears in cell E7. The loans with shorter terms have much higher payments. You will not know the entire financial picture until you calculate the total payments and total interest for each lender.

6. **Click cell F5, type =, click cell E5, type *, click cell D5, then press [Tab]; in cell G5, type =, click cell F5, type –, click cell B5, then click ✓**

> **QUICK TIP**
> You can evaluate and check for errors in worksheet formulas using the Formula Auditing toolbar. Right-click any toolbar and click Formula Auditing to display the toolbar.

7. **Copy the formulas in cells F5:G5 into the range F6:G7, then return to cell A1**
   Compare your results with those in Figure E-17. You can experiment with different interest rates, loan amounts, or terms for any one of the lenders; the PMT function generates a new set of values automatically.

8. **Enter your name in cell A13, save the workbook, then preview and print the worksheet**

FIGURE E-15: Example of PMT function for car loan

$$PMT(\underline{0.085/12},\underline{60},\underline{15000}) = \underline{\$307.75}$$

Interest rate per period (rate)   Number of payments (nper)   Present value of loan amount (pv)   Monthly payment calculated

FIGURE E-16: PMT function calculating monthly loan payment

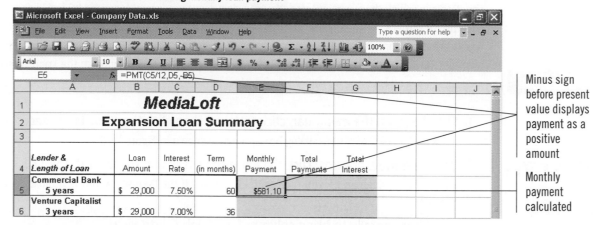

Minus sign before present value displays payment as a positive amount

Monthly payment calculated

FIGURE E-17: Completed worksheet

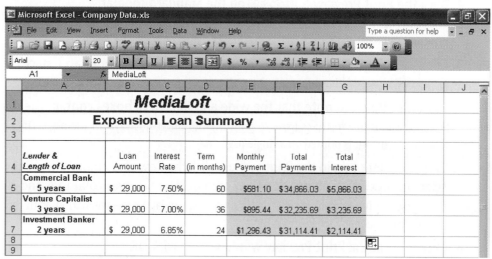

Clues to Use

Calculating future value with the FV function

You can use the FV (Future Value) function to determine the amount of money a given monthly investment will amount to, at a given interest rate after a given number of payment periods. The syntax is similar to that of the PMT function: FV(rate,nper,pmt,pv,type). For example, suppose you want to invest $1000 every month for the next 12 months into an account that pays 12% a year, and you want to know how much you will have at the end of 12 months (that is, its future value). You enter the function FV(.01,12,–1000), and Excel returns the value $12,682.50 as the future value of your investment. As with the PMT function, the units for the rate and nper must be consistent. If you made monthly payments on a three-year loan at 6% annual interest, you use the rate .06/12 and 36 periods (12*3). The arguments pv and type are optional; pv is the present value, or the total amount the series of payments is worth now. If you omit it, Excel assumes the pv is 0. The "type" argument indicates when the payments are made; 0 is the end of the period, and 1 is the beginning of the period.

Displaying and Printing Formula Contents

Excel usually displays the result of formula calculations in the worksheet area and displays formula contents for the active cell in the formula bar. However, you can instruct Excel to display the formulas directly in the worksheet cells in which they were entered. You can document worksheet formulas by first displaying the formulas, then printing them. These formula printouts are valuable paper-based worksheet documentation. Because formulas are often longer than their corresponding values, landscape orientation is the best choice for printing formulas. ▰▰▰▰▰ Jim wants you to produce a formula printout to submit with the Loan worksheet.

STEPS

1. **Click Tools on the menu bar, click Options, then click the View tab if necessary**

   The View tab of the Options dialog box appears, as shown in Figure E-18.

2. **Under Window options, click the Formulas check box to select it, then click OK**

   The columns widen and retain their original formats. If the Formula Auditing toolbar is displayed, you can close it.

   > **QUICK TIP**
   >
   > The worksheet formulas can also be displayed by selecting Formula Auditing Mode from the Formula Auditing option on the Tools menu.

3. **Scroll horizontally to bring columns E through G into view**

   Instead of displaying formula results in the cells, Excel shows the actual formulas and automatically adjusts the column widths to accommodate them.

4. **Click the Print Preview button 🔍 on the Standard toolbar**

   The status bar reads Preview: Page 1 of 2, indicating that the worksheet will print on two pages. You want to print it on one page and include the row number and column letter headings.

   > **QUICK TIP**
   >
   > All Page Setup options—such as Landscape orientation and Fit to scaling—apply to the active worksheet and are saved with the workbook.

5. **Click Setup in the Print Preview window, then click the Page tab if necessary**

6. **Under Orientation, click the Landscape option button; then under Scaling, click the Fit to option button and note that the wide and tall check boxes contain the number "1"**

   Selecting Landscape instructs Excel to print the worksheet sideways on the page. The Fit to option ensures that the document is printed on a single page.

   > **QUICK TIP**
   >
   > To print row and column labels on every page of a multiple-page worksheet, click the Sheet tab, and fill in the Rows to repeat at top and the Columns to repeat at left in the Print titles section.

7. **Click the Sheet tab, in the Print section, click the Row and column headings check box to select it, click OK, then position the Zoom pointer 🔍 over column A and click**

   The worksheet formulas now appear on a single page, in landscape orientation, with row (number) and column (letter) headings. See Figure E-19.

8. **Click Print in the Print Preview window, then click OK**

   After you retrieve the printout, you want to return the worksheet to displaying formula results. You can do this easily by using a key combination.

9. **Press [Ctrl][`] to redisplay formula results**

   [Ctrl][`] (grave accent mark) toggles between displaying formula results and displaying formula contents.

10. **Save the workbook, then close it and exit Excel**

   The completed payroll worksheet is displayed in Figure E-3; the completed sales worksheet is displayed in Figure E-7; the completed invoice worksheet is shown in Figure E-14, and the completed loan worksheets are displayed in Figures E-17 and E-19.

FIGURE E-18: View tab of the Options dialog box

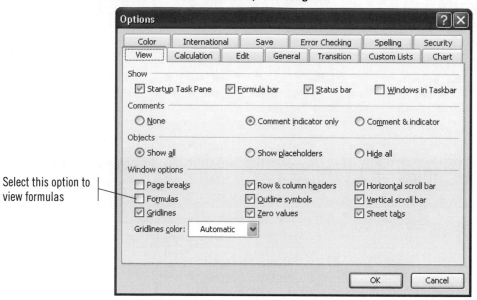

Select this option to view formulas

FIGURE E-19: Print Preview window

Column headings

Row headings

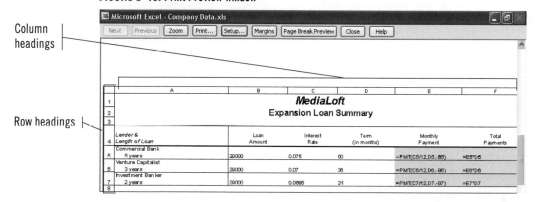

Clues to Use

Setting margins and alignment when printing part of a worksheet

You can set custom margins to print smaller sections of a worksheet. Select the range you want to print, click File on the menu bar, click Print, in the Print what section click Selection, then click Preview. In the Print Preview window, click Setup, then click the Margins tab. See Figure E-20. Double-click the margin numbers and type new ones. Use the Center on page check boxes to center the range horizontally or vertically. If you plan to print the range again, save the view after you print: click View on the menu bar, click Custom Views, click Add, then type a view name and click OK.

FIGURE E-20: Margins tab in the Page Setup dialog box

Practice

▼ CONCEPTS REVIEW

FIGURE E-21

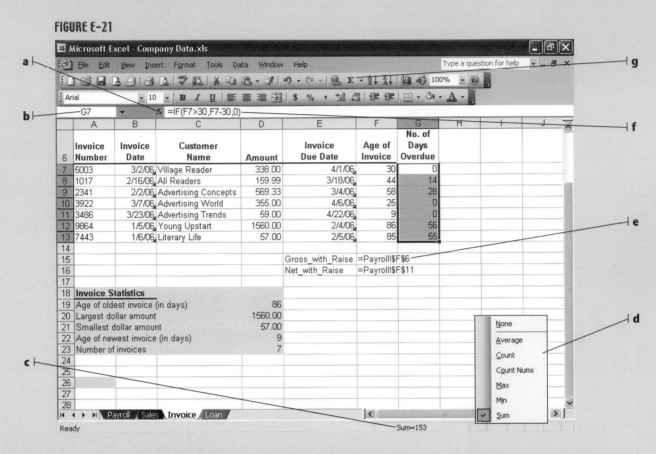

1. Which element points to the area where a name is assigned to a cell?
2. Which element points to a conditional formula?
3. Which element points to the AutoCalculate options?
4. Which element points to a list of the names assigned in the worksheet?
5. Which element do you click to insert a function into a worksheet?
6. Which element points to the result of an AutoCalculate option?
7. Which element do you click to enter a total of adjacent values into a blank cell?

Match each term with the statement that best describes it.

8. Style
9. COUNTA
10. test_cond
11. COUNT
12. pv

a. Function used to count the number of nonblank entries
b. A combination of formatting characteristics
c. Part of the PMT function that represents the loan amount
d. Part of the IF function in which the conditions are stated
e. Function used to count the number of numerical entries

Select the best answer from the list of choices.

13. **To generate a positive payment value when using the PMT function, you must:**
    a. Enter the function arguments as positive values.
    b. Enter the function arguments as negative values.
    c. Enter the interest rate divisor as a negative value.
    d. Enter the amount being borrowed as a negative value.

14. **When you enter the rate and nper arguments in a PMT function, you must:**
    a. Be consistent in the units used.
    b. Multiply both units by 12.
    c. Divide both values by 12.
    d. Use monthly units instead of annual units.

15. **To express conditions such as less than or equal to, you can use a(n):**
    a. Statistical function.
    b. PMT function.
    c. AutoCalculate formula.
    d. Comparison operator.

16. **Which of the following statements is false?**
    a. You can use only existing number and date formats in Excel.
    b. You can create custom number and date formats in Excel.
    c. Dates are stored in Excel as serial numbers.
    d. m/d/yy is an Excel date format.

▼ SKILLS REVIEW

1. **Create a formula with several operators.**
   a. Start Excel, open the Data File EX E-2.xls from the drive and folder where your Data Files are stored, then save the workbook as **Manager Bonuses**.
   b. On the Bonuses worksheet, select cell C13 using the Go To command.
   c. Enter the formula **.2*AVERAGE(C4:C10)**.
   d. Enter the formula **.1*C13** in cell **C14**.
   e. Use the Paste Special command to paste the values and formats in B4:B10 to G4:G10, then save your work.

2. **Use names in a formula.**
   a. Name cell C13 **Dept_Bonus**.
   b. Name cell C14 **Project_Bonus**.
   c. Select the range C4:C10 and name it **Base_Pay**.
   d. In cell E4, enter the formula **Dept_Bonus*D4+Project_Bonus**.
   e. Copy the formula in cell E4 into the range E5:E10.
   f. Format range E4:E10 with the Comma style, using the Style dialog box.
   g. Select the range E4:E10, if necessary, and name it **Bonus_Total**.
   h. In cell F4, enter a formula that sums Base_Pay and Bonus_Total.
   i. Copy the formula in cell F4 into the range F5:F10.
   j. Format range F4:F10 with the Comma style, using the Style dialog box.
   k. Save your work.

3. **Generate multiple totals with AutoSum.**
   a. Select range E4:F11.
   b. Enter the totals using AutoSum.
   c. Check the formulas in cells E11:F11 to make sure they are correct.
   d. Format range E11:F11 with the Currency style, using the Style dialog box.
   e. Enter your name in cell A18, save your work, then preview and print this worksheet.

4. Use dates in calculations.

   a. Make the Merit Pay sheet active.

   b. In cell D6, enter the formula **B6+183**.

   c. Copy the formula in cell D6 into the range D7:D14.

   d. Use the NOW function to insert the date and time in cell A3.

   e. In cell E18, enter the text **Last Pay Date for Year**, and in cell G18, use the Date function to enter the date **12/31/2006**.

   f. Save your work.

5. Build a conditional formula with the IF function.

   a. In cell F6, use the Function dialog box to enter the formula **IF(C6=5,E6*0.05,0)**.

   b. Copy the formula in cell F6 into the range F7:F14.

   c. Make sure the total in cell F15 is correct.

   d. Apply the Comma style with no decimal places to F6:F14.

   e. Save your work.

6. Use statistical functions.

   a. In cell C19, enter a function to calculate the average salary in the range E6:E14.

   b. In cell C20, enter a function to calculate the largest bonus in the range F6:F14.

   c. In cell C21, enter a function to calculate the lowest performance rating in the range C6:C14.

   d. In cell C22, enter a function to calculate the number of entries in range A6:A14.

   e. Apply the Comma style with no decimal places to C19:C22. Compare your results with Figure E-22.

   f. Enter your name into cell A28, then save, preview, and print the worksheet.

FIGURE E-22

18	Department Statistics	
19	Average Salary	30,560
20	Highest Bonus	1,825
21	Lowest Performance Rating	3
22	Number of Employees	9
23		
24		
25		
26		
27		
28		
29		
30		

Bonuses / **Merit Pay** / Loan /

Ready

7. Calculate payments with the PMT function.

   a. Make the Loan sheet active.

   b. In cell B9, use the Insert Function dialog box to enter the formula **PMT(B5/12,B6,-B4)**.

   c. In cell B10, enter the formula **B9*B6**.

   d. AutoFit column B, if necessary.

   e. In cell B11, enter the formula **B10-B4**.

   f. Enter your name in cell A15, then save, preview, and print the worksheet.

8. Display and print formula contents.

   a. Use the View tab in the Options dialog box to display formulas in the worksheet. If the Formula Auditing toolbar opens, you can close it.

   b. Adjust the column widths as necessary.

   c. Save, preview, and print this worksheet on one page in landscape orientation with the row and column headings.

   d. Redisplay the formula results in the worksheet, then resize columns as necessary.

   e. Close the workbook, then exit Excel.

▼ INDEPENDENT CHALLENGE 1

As manager of Mike's Ice Cream Parlor, you have been asked to create a worksheet that totals the monthly sales of all store products. Your monthly report should include the following:

- Sales totals for the current month for each product
- Sales totals for the last month for each product
- The percent change in sales from last month to this month

To document the report further, you decide to include a printout of the worksheet formulas.

a. Start Excel, open the Data File EX E-3.xls from the drive and folder where your Data Files are stored, then save it as **Mike's Sales**.
b. Use the TODAY function to enter today's date in cell A3.
c. Create and apply a custom format for the date entry.
d. Use AutoSum to enter totals for each week, and current month totals for each product.
e. Calculate the percent change in sales from the previous month for regular ice cream. (*Hint*: The formula in words would be (Current Month-Last Month)/Last Month.)
f. Copy the percent change formula down the column for the other products using AutoFill, then format the column with the Percent style using the Formatting toolbar.
g. Apply a Comma style with no decimal places to all weekly figures and totals, using the Formatting toolbar.
h. Enter your name into cell A15, then save, preview, and print the worksheet on a single page.
i. Display and preview the worksheet formulas, then print the formulas in landscape orientation on one page with row and column headings.
j. Close the workbook without saving the changes for displaying formulas, then exit Excel.

▼ INDEPENDENT CHALLENGE 2

You are an auditor with a certified public accounting firm. Fly Away, a manufacturer of skating products, has contacted you to audit its financial records. The management at Fly Away is considering opening a branch in Great Britain and needs its records audited to prepare the business plan. The managers at Fly Away have asked you to assist them in preparing their year-end sales summary as part of this audit. Specifically, they want to add expenses and show the percent of annual expenses that each expense category represents. They also want to show what percent of annual sales each expense category represents. You will include a formula calculating the difference between sales and expenses and another formula calculating expenses divided by sales. The expense categories and their respective dollar amounts are as follows: Building Lease $50,000; Equipment $208,000; Office $25,000; Salary $355,000; Taxes $310,000. Use these expense amounts to prepare the year-end sales and expenses summary for Fly Away.

a. Start Excel, open the Data File EX E-4.xls from the drive and folder where your Data Files are stored, then save the workbook as **Fly Away Sales**.
b. Name the cell containing the formula for total annual expenses **Annual_Expenses**. Use the name Annual_Expenses in cell C12 to create a formula calculating percent of annual expenses. Copy this formula as necessary and apply the Percent style. Add a formula that sums all the values for percent of annual expenses, which should equal 100%.
c. In cell D12, enter a formula calculating the percent of annual sales each expense category represents. Use the name **Annual_Sales** in the formula (cell B9 has been named Annual_Sales). Copy this formula as necessary and apply the Percent style. Include a formula that sums all the values for percent of annual sales.
d. Enter the formula calculating Net Profit in cell B19, using the names Annual_Sales and Annual_Expenses.
e. Enter the formula for Expenses as a percent of sales in cell B20, using the names Annual_Sales and Annual_Expenses.
f. Format cell B19 as Currency with two decimal places. Format cell B20 using the Percentage style with two decimal places. Widen the columns as necessary to display cell contents.
g. Enter your name into cell A22.

▼ INDEPENDENT CHALLENGE 2 (CONTINUED)

Advanced Challenge Exercise

- Display the Formula Auditing toolbar and check the worksheet for errors.
- Use the Formula Auditing toolbar to evaluate the formula in cell B20.
- Close the Formula Auditing toolbar.

h. Save, preview, and print the worksheet.

i. Close the workbook, then exit Excel.

▼ INDEPENDENT CHALLENGE 3

As the owner of Custom Fit, a general contracting firm specializing in home-storage projects, you are facing a business challenge at your firm. Because jobs are taking longer than expected, you decide to take out a $10,000 loan to purchase some new power tools. You check three loan sources: the Small Business Administration (SBA), your local bank, and a consortium of investors. The SBA will lend you the money at 7% interest, but you have to pay it off in three years. The local bank offers you the loan at 7.75% interest over four years. The consortium offers you a 6.75% loan, but they require you to pay it back in two years. To analyze all three loan options, you decide to build a loan summary worksheet. Using the loan terms provided, build a worksheet summarizing your options.

a. Start Excel, open a new workbook, then save it as **Custom Fit Loan Options** in the drive and folder where your Data Files are stored.

b. Enter today's date in cell A3, using the TODAY function.

c. Using Figure E-23 as a guide, enter labels and worksheet data for the three loan sources.

FIGURE E-23

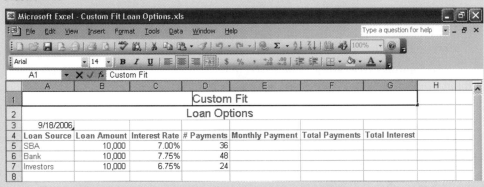

d. Enter the monthly payment formula for your first loan source (making sure to show the payment as a positive amount), copy the formula as appropriate, then name the range containing the monthly payment formulas **Monthly_Payment**.

e. Name the cell range containing the number of payments, **Number_Payments**.

f. Enter the formula for total payments for your first loan source using the named ranges **Monthly_Payment** and **Number_Payments**, then copy the formula as necessary.

g. Name the cell range containing the formulas for Total payments, **Total_Payments**. Name the cell range containing the loan amounts, **Loan_Amount**.

h. Enter the formula for total interest for your first loan source using the named ranges **Total_Payments** and **Loan_Amount**, then copy the formula as necessary.

i. Format the worksheet using formatting appropriate to the worksheet purpose, then enter your name in cell A14.

Advanced Challenge Exercise

- Paste the range names for the worksheet starting in cell E9.
- Name the cell range C5:C7 as Interest_Rate. Name the range G5:G7 as Total_Interest.
- Delete the pasted list of names and paste the new list.

j. Save, preview, and print the worksheet on a single page. Print the worksheet formulas showing row and column headings using landscape orientation. Do not save the worksheet with the formula settings.

k. Close the workbook then exit Excel.

▼ INDEPENDENT CHALLENGE 4

You have been asked to research IRA rates for your company's human resources department. The company plans to deposit $4000 in the employees' accounts at the beginning of each year. You have been asked to research current rates at financial institutions. You will use the Web to find this information. You will use the rate information to determine the value of the deposited money after five years.

a. Open your browser, then go to the search engine of your choice and search for **IRA rates** in the search text box. Find IRA rates offered by three institutions for a $4000 deposit, then write down the institution name, the rate, and the minimum deposit in the table below.

b. Start Excel, open a new workbook, then save it as **IRA Rates** in the drive and folder where your Data Files are stored.

c. Enter the column headings, row headings, and, research results from the table below into your IRA Rates workbook.

IRA Worksheet

Institution	Rate	Minimum Deposit	Number of Years	Amount Deposited (Yearly)	Future Value
			5	4000	
			5	4000	
			5	4000	
Highest Rate					
Average Rate					
Highest Future Value					

d. Use the FV function to calculate the future value of a $4000 yearly deposit over 35 years for each institution, making sure it appears as a positive number. Assume that the payments are made at the beginning of the period, so the Type argument equals 1.

e. Use Excel functions to enter the highest rate, the average rate, and the highest future value into the workbook.

f. Enter your name in cell A15, then save, preview, and print the worksheet on a single page with one inch left and right margins.

g. Display and print the formulas for the worksheet on a single page using landscape orientation. Do not save the worksheet with the formulas displayed.

h. Close the workbook then exit Excel.

▼ VISUAL WORKSHOP

Create the worksheet shown in Figure E-24. (*Hints:* Use IF formulas to enter the bonus amounts. An employee with a performance rating of seven or higher receives a bonus of $1000. If the rating is less than seven, no bonus is awarded. The summary information in cells A15:C18 uses the SUM function and statistical functions.) Enter your name in cell A20, and save the workbook as **Bonus Pay**. Preview and then print the worksheet.

FIGURE E-24

Glossary

3-D reference A reference that uses values on other sheets or workbooks, effectively creating another dimension to a workbook.

Absolute cell reference A cell reference that contains a dollar sign before the column letter and/or row number to indicate the absolute, or fixed, contents of specific cells. For example, the formula $A$1+$B$1 calculates only the sum of these specific cells no matter where the formula is copied in the workbook.

Active cell The current location of the cell pointer.

Alignment The placement of cell contents; for example, left, center, or right.

Analyze To manipulate data, such as a list, with Excel or another tool.

AND condition A filtering feature that searches for records by specifying that all entered criteria must be matched.

Apply To open a document based on an Excel template.

Area chart A line chart in which each area is given a solid color or pattern to emphasize the relationship between the pieces of charted information.

Argument Information that a function needs to calculate an answer. In an expression, multiple arguments are separated by commas. All of the arguments are enclosed in parentheses; for example, =SUM(A1:B1).

Argument ScreenTip The yellow box that appears as you build a function. As you build the function using different elements, the box displays these elements. You can click each element to display its online help.

Arithmetic operator A symbol used in a formula (such as + or -, /, or *) to perform mathematical operations.

ASCII file A text file that contains data but no formatting; instead of being divided into columns, ASCII file data are separated, or delimited, by tabs or commas.

Ascending order In sorting worksheet records, the order that begins with the letter A or the number 1.

Attribute The styling features such as bold, italics, and underlining that can be applied to cell contents. In XML, the component that provides information about the document's elements.

Auditing An Excel feature that helps track errors and check worksheet logic.

AutoCalculate value Value displayed in the status bar that represents the sum of values in the selected range.

AutoComplete A feature that automatically completes entries based on other entries in the same column.

AutoFill A feature that creates a series of text entries or numbers when a range is selected using the fill handle.

AutoFill Options button Allows you to specify what you want to fill and whether or not you want to include formatting.

AutoFilter An Excel list feature that lets you click a list arrow and select criteria by which to display certain types of records.

AutoFilter list arrows Small triangles that appear next to field names in an Excel list; used to display portions of your data.

AutoFit A feature that automatically adjusts the width of a column to accommodate its widest entry when the boundary to the right of the column selector is double-clicked.

AutoFormat Preset schemes that can be applied to format a range instantly. Excel comes with 16 AutoFormats that include colors, fonts, and numeric formatting.

AutoSum A feature that automatically creates totals using the SUM function when you click the AutoSum button.

Background color The color applied to the background of a cell.

Backsolving A problem-solving method in which you specify a solution and then find the input value that produces the answer you want; sometimes described as a what-if analysis in reverse. In Excel, the Goal Seek feature performs backsolving.

Bar chart A chart that shows information as a series of horizontal bars.

Border The edge of a cell, an area of a worksheet, or a selected object; you can change its color or line style.

Bug In programming, an error that causes a procedure to run incorrectly.

Category axis The x-axis (horizontal axis) of a chart.

Cell The intersection of a column and row in a worksheet, datasheet, or table.

Cell address The location of a cell expressed by the column and row coordinates; the cell address of the cell in column A, row 1, is A1.

Cell comments Notes you've written about a workbook that appear when you place the pointer over a cell.

Cell pointer A highlighted rectangle around a cell that indicates the active cell.

Cell reference The address or name that identifies a cell's position in a worksheet; it consists of a letter that identifies the cell's column and a number that identifies its row; for example, cell B3. Cell references in worksheets can be used in formulas and are relative or absolute. *See also* Absolute cell reference and Relative cell reference.

Change history A worksheet containing a list of changes made to a shared workbook.

Changing cells In what-if analysis, cells that contain the values that change in order to produce multiple sets of results.

Chart A graphic representation of worksheet information. Types include 2-D and 3-D column, bar, pie, area, and line charts.

Chart sheet A separate sheet that contains only a chart linked to worksheet data.

Chart Wizard A series of dialog boxes that helps you create or modify a chart.

Clip An individual media file, such as art, sound, animation, or a movie.

Clip art An image such as a corporate logo, a picture, or a photo.

Clipboard A temporary storage area for cut or copied items that are available for pasting. *See also* Office Clipboard.

Clipboard task pane A task pane that shows the contents of the Office Clipboard; contains options for copying and pasting items.

Code *See* Program Code.

Code window In the Visual Basic Editor, the window that displays the selected module's procedures, written in the Visual Basic programming language.

Column chart The default chart type in Excel, which displays information as a series of vertical columns.

Column heading The gray box containing the letter above the column in a worksheet.

Combination chart Combines a column and line chart to compare data requiring different scales of measure.

Comments In a Visual Basic procedure, notes that explain the purpose of the macro or procedure; they are preceded by a single apostrophe and appear in green. *See also* cell comments.

Complex formula An equation that uses more than one type of arithmetic operator.

Conditional format A cell format that is based on the cell's value or the outcome of a formula.

Conditional formula A formula that makes calculations based on stated conditions, such as calculating a rebate based on a particular purchase amount.

Consolidate To combine data on multiple worksheets and display the result on another worksheet.

Control menu box A box in the upper-left corner of a window used to resize or close a window.

Criteria Conditions that must be met when searching for files.

Criteria range A cell range containing one row of labels (usually a copy of column labels) and at least one additional row underneath it that contains the criteria you want to match.

Custom chart type A specially formatted Excel chart.

Data entry area The unlocked portion of a worksheet where users are able to enter and change data.

Data form In an Excel list (or database), a dialog box that displays one record at a time.

Data label Descriptive text that appears above a data marker in a chart.

Data marker A graphical representation of a data point, such as a bar or column.

Data point Individual piece of data plotted in a chart.

Data series The selected range in a worksheet that Excel converts into a graphic and displays as a chart.

Data table A range of cells that shows the resulting values when one or more input values are varied in a formula; when one input value is changed, the table is called a one-input data table, and when two input values are changed, it is called a two-input data table. In a chart it is a grid containing the chart data.

Data validation A feature that allows you to specify what data is allowable (valid) for a range of cells.

Database An organized collection of related information. In Excel, a database is called a list.

Debug In programming, to find and correct an error in code.

Declare In the Visual Basic programming language, assigning a type, such as numeric or text, to a variable.

Delimiter A tab or space used in text files to separate columns of data.

Dependent cell A cell, usually containing a formula, whose value changes depending on the values in the input cells. For example, a payment formula or function that depends on an input cell containing changing interest rates is a dependent cell.

Descending order In sorting an Excel list, the order that begins with the letter Z or the highest number in a list.

Destination program In a data exchange, the program that will receive the data.

Document To make notes about basic worksheet assumptions, complex formulas, or questionable data. In a macro, to insert comments that explain the Visual Basic code.

Drag-and-drop technique Method in which you drag the contents of selected cells to a new location.

Dummy column/row Blank column or row included at the end of a range that enables a formula to adjust when columns or rows are added or deleted.

Dynamic page breaks In a larger workbook, horizontal or vertical dashed lines that represent the place where pages print separately. They also adjust automatically when you insert or delete rows or columns, or change column widths or row heights.

Electronic spreadsheet A computer program that performs calculations on data and organizes information into worksheets. A worksheet is divided into columns and rows, which form individual cells.

Element An XML component that defines the document content.

Embedded chart A chart displayed as an object in a worksheet.

Embedding Inserting a copy of data into a destination document; you can double-click the embedded object to modify it using the tools of the source program.

Exploding pie slice A slice of a pie chart that has been pulled away from the whole pie to add emphasis.

Extensible Markup Language (XML) A system for defining languages using tags to structure data.

External reference indicator The exclamation point (!) used in a formula to indicate that a referenced cell is outside the active sheet.

Extract To place a copy of a filtered list in a range you specify in the Advanced Filter dialog box.

Field In a list (an Excel database), a column that describes a characteristic about records, such as first name or city.

Field name A column label that describes a field.

File properties Attributes of a file, such as author name, file size, and file type.

Fill color The cell background color.

Fill handle A small square in the lower-right corner of the active cell used to copy cell contents.

Filter To display data in an Excel list that meet specified criteria.

Font The typeface or design of a set of characters.

Font size The size of characters, measured in units called points (pts).

Footer Information that prints at the bottom of each printed page; on screen, a footer is visible only in Print Preview.

Format The appearance of text and numbers, including color, font, attributes, borders, and shading. *See also* Number format.

Format Painter A feature used to copy the formatting applied to one set of text or in one cell to another.

Formatting toolbar A toolbar that contains buttons for frequently used formatting commands.

Formula A set of instructions used to perform numeric calculations (adding, multiplying, averaging, etc.).

Formula bar The area below the menu bar and above the Excel workspace where you enter and edit data in a worksheet cell. The formula bar becomes active when you start typing or editing cell data. It includes the Enter button and the Cancel button.

Formula prefix An arithmetic symbol, such as the equal sign (=), used to start a formula.

Freeze To hold in place selected columns or rows when scrolling in a worksheet that is divided in panes. *See also* panes.

Function A special, predefined formula that provides a shortcut for a commonly used calculation; for example, AVERAGE.

Getting Started task pane Lets you quickly open new or existing workbooks.

Goal cell In backsolving, a cell containing a formula in which you can substitute values to find a specific value, or goal.

Goal Seek A problem-solving method in which you specify a solution and then find the input value that produces the answer you want; sometimes described as a what-if analysis in reverse; also called backsolving.

Gridlines Horizontal and/or vertical lines within a chart that make the chart easier to read.

Header Information that prints at the top of each printed page; on screen, a header is visible only in Print Preview.

Help system A utility that gives you immediate access to definitions, steps, explanations, and useful tips.

Hide To make rows, columns, formulas, or sheets invisible to workbook users.

Hotspot An object that, when clicked, will run a macro or open a file.

HTML Hypertext Markup Language, the format of pages that a Web browser such as Internet Explorer or Netscape Navigator can read.

Hyperlink An object (a filename, a word, a phrase, or a graphic) in a worksheet that, when you click it, will display another worksheet or a Web page called the target.

If...Then...Else statement In the Visual Basic programming language, a conditional statement that directs Excel to perform specified actions under certain conditions; its syntax is "If *condition* Then *statements* Else [*elsestatements*]".

Input Information that produces desired results, or output, in a worksheet.

Input cells Spreadsheet cells that contain data instead of formulas and that act as input to a what-if analysis; input values often change to produce different results. Examples include interest rates, prices, or other data.

Insert row The last row in an Excel list, where a record can be entered.

Insertion point The blinking vertical line that appears in the formula bar or in a cell during editing in Excel.

Integration A process where data is exchanged among Excel and other Windows programs; can include pasting, importing, exporting, embedding, and linking.

Interactivity A feature of a worksheet saved as an HTML document and posted to an intranet or Web site that allows users to manipulate data using their browsers.

Intranet An internal network site used by a particular group of people who work together.

Keyword A representative word on which the Help system can search to find information on your area of interest. In a macro procedure, words that are recognized as part of the Visual Basic programming language.

Label Descriptive text or other information that identifies the rows and columns of a worksheet. Labels are not included in calculations.

Label prefix A character, such as the apostrophe, that identifies an entry as a label and controls the way it appears in the cell.

Landscape orientation A print setting that positions the worksheet on the page so the page is wider than it is tall.

Legend A key explaining how information is represented by colors or patterns in a chart.

Line chart A graph of data that is mapped by a series of lines. Line charts show changes in data or categories of data over time and can be used to document trends.

Linking Inserting an object into a destination program; The information you insert will be updated automatically when the data in the source document changes.

List The Excel term for a database, an organized collection of related information.

Lock To secure a row, column, or sheet so that data in that location cannot be changed.

Logical condition A filtering feature that searches for records using And and Or conditions; the conditions can include operators such as greater than or less than.

Logical test The first part of an IF function; if the logical test is true, then the second part of the function is applied, and if it is false, then the third part of the function is applied.

Macro A set of instructions recorded or written in the Visual Basic programming language used to automate worksheet tasks.

Main procedure A procedure containing several macros that run sequentially.

Manual calculation option An option that turns off automatic calculation of worksheet formulas, allowing you to selectively determine if and when you want Excel to perform calculations.

Map An XML schema that is attached to a workbook.

Map an XML element A process where XML element names are placed on an Excel worksheet in a specific locations.

Menu bar The bar beneath the title bar that contains the names of menus, that when clicked, open menus from which you choose program commands.

Minor gridlines Gridlines that show the values between the tick marks.

Mixed reference A formula containing both a relative and absolute reference.

Mode indicator A box located in the lower-left corner of the status bar that informs you of a program's status. For example, when Excel is performing a task, the word "Wait" appears.

Model A worksheet used to produce a what-if analysis that acts as the basis for multiple outcomes.

Module In Visual Basic, a module is stored in a workbook and contains macro procedures.

Moving border The dashed line that appears around a cell or range that is copied to the Clipboard.

Name box The left-most area in the formula bar that shows the cell reference or name of the active cell. For example, A1 refers to cell A1 of the active worksheet. You can also display a list of names in a workbook using the Name list arrow.

Named range A range of cells given a meaningful name; it retains its name when moved and can be referenced in a formula.

Number format A format applied to values to express numeric concepts, such as currency, date, and percentage.

Object A chart or graphic image that can be moved and resized and contains handles when selected. In object linking and embedding (OLE), the data to be exchanged between another document or program. In Visual Basic, every Excel element, including ranges.

Object Linking and Embedding (OLE) A Microsoft Windows technology that allows you to transfer data from one document and program to another using embedding or linking.

Office Clipboard A temporary storage area shared by all Office programs that can be used to cut, copy and paste multiple items within and between Office programs. The Office Clipboard can hold up to 24 items collected from any Office program. *See also* Clipboard and Clipboard task pane.

OLE *See* Object Linking and Embedding.

One-input data table A range of cells that shows resulting values when one input value in a formula is changed.

Order of precedence The order in which Excel calculates parts of a formula: (1) operations in parentheses (2) exponents, (3) multiplication and division, and (4) addition and subtraction.

Outline symbols In outline view, the buttons that, when clicked, changes the amount of detail in the outlined worksheet.

Output The end result of a worksheet.

Page field In a PivotTable or a PivotChart report, a field area that lets you view data as if it is stacked in pages, effectively adding a third dimension to the data analysis.

Panes Sections into which you can divide a worksheet when you want to work on separate parts of the worksheet at the same time; one pane freezes, or remains in place, while you scroll in another pane until you see the desired information.

Paste Function A series of dialog boxes that helps you build functions; it lists and describes all Excel functions.

Personal macro workbook A workbook that can contain macros that are available to any open workbook. By default, the personal macro workbook is hidden.

Pie chart A circular chart that represents data as slices of a pie. A pie chart is useful for showing the relationship of parts to a whole; pie slices can be extracted for emphasis. *See also* Exploding pie slice.

PivotChart report An Excel feature that lets you summarize worksheet data in the form of a chart in which you can rearrange, or "pivot," parts of the chart structure to explore new data relationships.

PivotTable Field List A window containing fields that can be used to create or modify a PivotTable.

PivotTable list An interactive PivotTable on a Web or intranet site that lets users explore data relationships using their browsers.

PivotTable report An Excel feature that allows you to summarize worksheet data in the form of a table in which you can rearrange, or "pivot," parts of the table structure to explore new data relationships; also called a PivotTable.

PivotTable toolbar Contains buttons that allow you to manipulate data in a PivotTable.

Plot area The area of a chart that contains the chart itself, its axes, and the legend.

Point A unit of measure used for fonts and row height. One inch equals 72 points, or a point is equal to ½ of an inch.

Pointing method Specifying formula cell references by selecting the desired cell with the mouse instead of typing its cell reference; it eliminates typing errors. Also known as Pointing.

Populate a worksheet with XML data The process of importing an XML file and filling the mapped elements on the worksheet with data from the XML file.

Portrait orientation A print setting that positions the worksheet on the page so the page is taller than it is wide.

Post To place an interactive workbook in a shared location.

Precedents In formula auditing, the cells that are used in the formula to calculate the value of a given cell.

Presentation graphics program A program such as Microsoft PowerPoint that you can use to create slide show presentations.

Preview A view of the worksheet exactly as it will appear on paper.

Primary Key The field in a database that contains unique information for each record.

Print area A portion of a worksheet that you can define using the Print Area command on the File menu; after you define a print area, clicking the Print icon on the Standard toolbar prints only that worksheet area.

Print title In a list that spans more than one page, the field names that print at the top of every printed page.

Procedure A sequence of Visual Basic statements contained in a macro that accomplishes a specific task.

Procedure footer In Visual Basic, the last line of a Sub procedure.

Procedure header The first line in a Visual Basic procedure.

Program Task-oriented software (such as Excel or Word) that enables you to perform a certain type of task, such as data calculation or word processing.

Program code Macro instructions, written in the Visual Basic for Applications programming language.

Project In the Visual Basic Editor, the equivalent of a workbook; a project contains Visual Basic modules.

Project Explorer In the Visual Basic Editor, a window that lists all open projects (or workbooks) and the worksheets and modules they contain.

Property In Visual Basic, an attribute of an object that describes its character or behavior.

Properties window In the Visual Basic Editor, the window that displays a list of characteristics, or properties, associated with a module.

Publish To place an Excel workbook or worksheet on a Web site or an intranet in HTML format so that others can access it using their Web browsers.

Range
A selected group of adjacent cells.

Range finder A feature that outlines an equation's arguments in blue and green.

Range object In Visual Basic, an object that represents a cell or a range of cells.

Record In a list (an Excel database), data about an object or a person.

Refresh To update a PivotTable so it reflects changes to the underlying data.

Relative cell reference A type of cell reference used to indicate a relative position in the worksheet. It allows you to copy and move formulas from one area to another of the same dimensions. Excel automatically changes the column and row numbers to reflect the new position. Also known as Relative reference.

Research services Reference information available through the Research task pane that can be inserted into your document.

Retrieve In Autofilter, to search for and list records.

Route To send an e-mail attachment sequentially to each user in a list, who then forwards it to the next user on the list.

Routing slip A list of e-mail users who are to receive an e-mail attachment.

Row height The vertical dimension of a cell.

Row heading The gray box containing the row number to the left of the row.

Run To play, as a macro.

Scenario
A set of values you use to forecast results; the Excel Scenario Manager lets you store and manage different scenarios.

Scenario summary An Excel table that compiles data from various scenarios so that you can view the scenario results next to each other for easy comparison.

Schema In an XML document, a list of the fields, called elements or attributes, and their characteristics.

Search criterion The specification for data that you want to find in an Excel list, such as "Brisbane" or "is greater than 1000."

Series of labels Preprogrammed series, such as days of the week and months of the year. They are formed by typing the first word of the series, then dragging the fill handle to select and fill the desired range of cells.

Shared workbook An Excel workbook that several users can open and modify.

Sheet A term used for a worksheet.

Sheet tab A description at the bottom of each worksheet that identifies it in a workbook. In an open workbook, move to a worksheet by clicking its sheet tab. Also known as Worksheet tab.

Sheet tab scrolling buttons Buttons that enable you to move among sheets within a workbook.

Single-file Web page A Web page that integrates all of the worksheets and graphical elements from a workbook into a single file in the MHTML file format, making it easier to publish to the Web. Users who have IE 4.0 or higher can open a Web page saved in MHTML format.

Sizing handles Small boxes appearing along the corners and sides of charts and graphic images that are used for moving and resizing.

Sort To change the order of records in a list according to one or more fields, such as Last Name.

Sort keys Criteria on which a sort, or a reordering of data, is based.

Source list The list on which a PivotTable is based.

Source program In a data exchange, the program used to create the data you are embedding or linking.

Standard chart type A commonly used column, bar, pie, or area chart in the Excel program; each type has several variations. For example, a column chart variation is the Columns with Depth.

Standard toolbar A toolbar that contains buttons for frequently used operating and editing commands.

Statement In Visual Basic, a line of code.

Status bar The bar at the bottom of the Excel window that provides information about various keys, commands, and processes.

Style A named combination of formatting characteristics, such as bold, italic, and zero decimal places.

Sub procedure A series of Visual Basic statements that performs an action but does not return a value.

SUM The most frequently used function, this adds columns or rows of cells.

Summary function In a PivotTable, a function that determines the type of calculation applied to the PivotTable data, such as SUM or COUNT.

Syntax In the Visual Basic programming language, the formatting rules that must be followed so that the macro will run correctly.

Table In an Access database, a list of data. In Excel, a special list containing worksheet data that can be searched using Excel features.

Target The location that a hyperlink displays after you click it.

Target cell In what-if analysis (specifically, in Excel Solver), the cell containing the formula.

Task pane A window area to the right of the worksheet that provides worksheet options, such as creating a new workbook, conducting a search, inserting Clip Art, and using the Office Clipboard.

Task pane list arrow Lets you switch between 11 different task panes.

Template A workbook containing text, formulas, macros, and formatting you use repeatedly; when you create a new document, you can open a document based on the template workbook. The new document will automatically contain the formatting, text, formulas, and macros in the template.

Text annotations Labels added to a chart to draw attention to a particular area.

Text color The color applied to text in a cell or on a chart.

Text file A file that consists of text but no formatting. It is also called an ASCII file.

Tick marks Notations of a scale of measure on a chart axis.

Title bar The bar at the top of the program window that indicates the program name and the name of the current file.

Toggle button A button that turns a feature on and off.

Toolbar A bar that contains buttons that you can click to perform commands.

Toolbar Options button A button you click on a toolbar to view toolbar buttons not currently visible.

Tracers In Excel worksheet auditing, arrows that point from cells that might have caused an error to the active cell containing an error.

Track To identify and keep a record of who makes which changes to a workbook.

Trendline A chart that represents trends in a data series.

Truncate To shorten the display of cell information because a cell is too wide.

Two-input data table A range of cells that shows resulting values when two input values in a formula are changed.

Type a question for help box Area on the menu bar in which you can query the Excel help system by typing a question.

URL *See* Uniform Resource Locator.

Uniform Resource Locator (URL) A unique Web address that identifies a Web page.

Validation *See* Data Validation.

Validation Circles In formula auditing, the circles that identify invalid data.

Value A number, formula, or function used in calculations.

Value axis Also known as the y-axis in a 2-dimensional chart, this area often contains numerical values that help you interpret the size of chart elements. In a 3-dimensional chart, the z-axis.

Variable In the Visual Basic programming language, an area in memory in which you can temporarily store an item of information; variables are often declared in Dim statements such as *DimNameAsString*.

View A set of display or print settings that you can name and save for access at another time. You can save multiple views of a worksheet.

Virus Destructive software that can damage your computer files.

Visual Basic Editor A program that lets you display and edit macro code.

Visual Basic for Applications (VBA) A programming language used to create macros in Excel.

Web discussion Comments attached to an Excel worksheet that you will save as an HTML document, allowing people viewing your worksheet on the Web to review and reply to your comments.

Web query An Excel feature that lets you obtain data from a Web, Internet, or intranet site and places it in an Excel workbook for analysis.

What-if analysis A decision-making feature in which data is changed and formulas based on it are automatically recalculated.

Wildcard A special symbol you use in defining search criteria in the data form or Replace dialog box. The most common types of wildcards are the question mark (?), which stands for any single character, and the asterisk (*), which represents any group of characters.

Window A rectangular area of a screen where you view and work on the open file.

WordArt Specially formatted text, created using the WordArt button on the Drawing toolbar.

Workbook A collection of related worksheets contained within a single file.

Worksheet An electronic spreadsheet containing 256 columns by 65,536 rows.

Worksheet tab *See* Sheet tab.

Worksheet window Includes the tools that enable you to create and work with worksheets.

Workspace An Excel file with an .xlw extension containing information about the identity, view, and placement of a set of open workbooks. Instead of opening each workbook individually, you can open the workspace file instead.

X-axis The horizontal axis in a chart; because it often shows data categories, such as months, it is also called the category axis.

X-axis label A label describing a chart's x-axis.

XML (Extensible Markup Language) A system for defining languages using tags to structure data.

XY (scatter) chart Compares trends over uneven time or measurement intervals; used in scientific and engineering disciplines for trend spotting and extrapolation.

Y-axis The vertical axis in a chart; because it often shows numerical values in a 2-dimensional chart, it is also called the value axis.

Y-axis label A label describing the y-axis of a chart.

Zoom A feature that enables you to focus on a larger or smaller part of the worksheet in Print Preview.

Index